The

INTP
QUEST

INTPs' Search for Their Core Self,
Purpose, & Philosophy

Dr. A.J. Drenth

CONTENTS

Introduction 1

Part I: The INTP Personality

1. Introverted Thinking (Ti) 13
2. Extraverted Intuition (Ne) 19
3. Introverted Sensing (Si) 25
4. Extraverted Feeling (Fe) 35

Part II: INTPs & Purpose

5. Importance & Energy 47
6. Ideas & Purpose 53
7. The I-E Struggle 63

Part III: INTPs & Philosophy

8. Foundations 69
9. Philosophy & Religion 79
10. Irreducible Mind 87
11. Life & Evolution 97
12. Philosophical Types 105
13. Philosophical Paths 111

Part IV: Toward Integration

14. "Nothing More to Explore" 125

15. The Transition 137

16. Integration 143

Closing Remarks... 159

References & Resources... 163

INTRODUCTION

Human beings are fragile creatures. While our oversized brains have afforded us dominion over nature, our reflective faculties have also opened the door to myriad existential problems such as apathy, anxiety, loneliness, and nihilism, all of which are markedly absent in other species. And while none of us is exempt from the array of challenges associated with the human predicament, not everyone navigates them in the same way. Those endowed with a sunny or lighthearted temperament may respond by securing plenty of fun and novel experiences for themselves. Preferring not to be burdened by heavy or serious matters, they opt to live in the moment and savor life's manifold pleasures. By contrast, those of a more serious disposition take a less hedonistic approach. While they too aspire to enjoy life, they demand more from it than fun and games. Their desire is for life, especially their own lives, to have a deeper sense of meaning and import. They want a life that is significant and substantive—one that matters. Those who seek this sort of higher calling come in two basic types: dogmatists and seekers.

Dogmatists evince a sense of knowingness and conviction with respect to their calling. One gets the sense that they have never really doubted or scrutinized their beliefs, and that what they hold dear is not open to revision or questioning. In other words, dogmatists seem to embrace their calling in an uncritical or closed-minded fashion. They are strong in both will and conviction, but lacking when it comes to openness and critical thinking.

Seekers are the opposite. They suffer from no deficit of openness or critical thinking. In fact, others may see them as *thinking too much* and thereby making life unduly complicated. What seekers lack is strength of conviction and clarity in direction. In contrast to the dogmatist, identifying their life's calling doesn't happen quickly or easily. They are inhabited by doubt, perhaps feeling that things are too murky or complex to be known with full confidence or certainty. And while there are times they may feel they have finally found what they are looking for—their personal Holy Grail—it is rarely long before they start doubting or questioning their conclusions, which once again foists them back into seeking mode.

Seekers' doubting nature may prompt others to see them as timid, fickle, or unreliable. Indeed, from the dogmatist's perspective, perpetual doubt is apt to be construed as a sign of weakness, suggestive of a lack of resolve or commitment. Viewed more positively, we might characterize seekers as open-minded and critical thinkers who are *concerned with getting things right*. Before choosing their life's course, they want to ensure they have covered all their bases and explored all the relevant options. Since they only get one life to live, they need to assure themselves that they have done everything in their power to discern their best path. While seekers may not know exactly what they are seeking or where they are headed, they know they want something more out of life, and their job is to find it. It is this vague but potent intention that fuels their quest.

The INTP Quest

Of *The 16 Personality Types*, at least one of those types, the INTP, brings a seeker mentality to life. While INTPs' status as nuanced and critical thinkers rarely goes unrecognized, their seeking side is often overlooked. This is largely due to the fact that INTPs do most of their seeking inwardly, that is, *they seek by way of thinking*. They see the mind as their primary vehicle for advancing in their personal quest.

Prior to commencing their quest, INTPs may feel bored, restless, or have a vague sense of emptiness. Some may try to assuage these feelings through things like sex, drugs, relationships, or achievement. While these sorts of distractions may work temporarily, it is rarely long before INTPs' sense of emptiness and restlessness returns, often with greater intensity.

At some point, INTPs grow weary of running and decide to face the issue head on. They acknowledge and embrace their desire for a better life, one which is more meaningful, substantive, and purposeful. Their essential sentiment may resemble that of Henry David Thoreau, who famously scribed in *Walden*:

> "I went to the woods because I wished to live deliberately, to confront only the essential facts of life, and see if I could not learn what it had to teach, and not, when I came to die, discover that I had not lived. I did not wish to live what was not life, living is so dear; nor did I wish to practice resignation, unless it was quite necessary. I wanted to live deep and suck out all the marrow of life . . ."

In taking up their quest, INTPs strive to live intentionally, or as Thoreau suggests, *deliberately*. Rather than blindly following a prescribed or conventional path, they feel compelled to contemplate alternatives, including the possibility of blazing their own trail. They sense that failing to explore a breadth of options may cause them to miss out on what is most profound or significant about life. Recognizing life's brevity, they don't want to look back and discover they "had not lived."

Unfortunately, discerning their optimal path often takes far longer than they anticipate. It can take years, even decades, for them to reach their desired level of clarity. Some INTPs may worry they might never find what they are looking for, and that all of their explorations will have been for naught. They may even consider terminating their quest prematurely. Rather than continuing to endure the frustration of having no clear path, they may be tempted, in the spirit of the dogmatist, to simply pick a path. At least this might liberate them from their otherwise incurable vacillation and indecision. However attractive this option may at times seem, most INTPs conclude it is not really viable for them. Recognizing that their life path needs to be personally meaningful and authentic, they know that an arbitrary choice could never satisfy them in the long run. Their only real option then, is to persist in their quest.

INTPs may also take note of the rather ironic fact that their quest feels surprisingly meaningful in its own right. Indeed, it is the closest thing many INTPs have to an authentic calling. Of course, nearly all INTPs will reject the notion that the quest itself is their ultimate aim or destination. Functioning as a lifelong seeker seems too easy, like a cop-out. It can also seem rather absurd or unproductive, akin to a dog chasing its own tail.

The INTP quest is characterized by a perpetual state of tension and striving, a groping for something that seems frustratingly slippery and elusive. At times, they may feel they are getting close, that their life's calling is just around the corner. But before they know it, something goes awry, once again leaving them lost and confused. They must then pick themselves up and resume their quest, hoping that fate might smile on them the next time around.

But what is the ultimate aim of their quest? What is it, exactly, that they are seeking? Although many INTPs, especially those in the early phases of their journey, may be incapable of fully knowing or articulating what they are seeking, the INTP quest can be generally understood as aimed at two primary things: purpose and wisdom.

Purpose & Wisdom

Purpose is characterized by a sense of energy, importance, and intentionality. While it can be embraced on either an individual or collective basis, modern-day INTPs are apt to lean toward the former, conceiving purpose as a personal calling or vocation. In many cases, their quest for purpose is interlaced with their search for an optimal career. Repelled by the idea of a mundane or mediocre career, INTPs strive to ensure that their life's work incorporates their core interests and purpose.

At first blush, wisdom may seem like a more abstruse and esoteric concept than purpose. But if we boil it down, it simply means knowing how to live optimally. Hence, insofar as INTPs are questing for a better life, they can be seen as seekers of wisdom. This, in combination with their penchant for contemplative and speculative thinking, has compelled many typologists to nickname them "philosophers," which literally means "lovers of wisdom."

While purpose and wisdom are by no means mutually exclusive concepts, they do have different emphases. Those seeking a purpose are largely concerned with defining or clarifying their *identity* and *direction*. Purpose involves adopting a specific role and identifying a point of focus. Wisdom, by contrast, highlights the *balance* and *relationships among things*, thus evoking notions such as temperance and moderation. Unlike purpose, it says little about direction or identity, but speaks more to one's *way of being*, emphasizing how one lives rather than what one does. We might see purpose as focused more on "the ends," whereas wisdom underscores "the means."

In the first half of life, INTPs tend to prioritize purpose over wisdom. Their foremost goal is to define who they are, what they enjoy, and what they will do with their lives. While they may realize, at least on some level, the importance of living a balanced life, this is typically not their foremost concern. Their first order of business is to clarify their identity and purpose. In psychological parlance, they must *differentiate* before they *integrate*.

Clarity of Understanding

In questing for identity and purpose, INTPs spend much of their time working to clarify their understanding. They feel that if they can just come to the right understanding, one that properly captures their essential self and purpose, then everything else will fall into place. Unfortunately, many INTPs find this to be no small task, largely because of the sheer volume of information they try to assimilate. Not only do INTPs feel compelled to clarify their understanding of themselves, but also that of the world (or universe) at large. They must then synthesize these two understandings in order to discern their overarching purpose.

INTPs' search for understanding often proceeds along two parallel tracks: the psychological and the philosophical / religious. Psychologically, INTPs strive to hone their conception of their core self, including their personality, skills, interests, abilities, etc. Seeing the self as a sort of roadmap for action, self-knowledge becomes a prerequisite for discerning their purpose. Without a clear sense of self, selecting a purpose seems too random or arbitrary to the INTP, like shooting blindly at a target.

Philosophically, INTPs strive to comprehend the bigger picture of life, humanity, and the universe. They seek to understand, or at least clarify their position on, the ultimate nature of things. Is there a God? If so, what is its nature? What is the mind and what are its origins? Is it fundamentally different from matter? It is important to recognize that INTPs don't contemplate these "big questions" from a point of indifference. They know that the conclusions they draw from their philosophical investigations will carry significant personal implications. Their beliefs about God, the universe, and humanity will affect how INTPs view themselves and their purpose.

Although INTPs may study psychology, philosophy, or religion on an independent basis, these subjects are by no means unrelated, especially in the mind of the INTP. Each of these disciplines strives to understand human beings and the human condition, as well as potential paths to the "good life." INTPs thus see them as invaluable companions in their quest for wisdom and understanding.

The Foundational Role of Type

INTPs don't necessarily get to choose their purpose. Emerging from the depths of their core self, their purpose in many respects *chooses them*. And because their personality type comprises a substantial part of their core self, their purpose can be seen as largely rooted in, and informed by, their type.

In my research and experience, I have observed profound psychological and behavioral similarities among INTPs, leading me to believe that INTPs don't really choose who they are or how they operate.[1] Rather they can be seen as following a sort of inner script, that of their type, which operates behind the scenes of their consciousness and undergirds the similarities of attitude, behavior, and ideation we observe among INTPs.[2] Because of the depth of insight and self-understanding furnished by typology, it can serve as a valuable tool and interpretive lens for the INTP quest.[3]

The Nature of this Book

INTPs feel called to a better life. This compels them to embark on a quest for purpose, wisdom, and understanding. As we've seen, INTPs see the mind as their primary vehicle for advancing in this quest. They sense that it is only by clarifying their understanding that they can zero-in on their true purpose. And it is toward this end that this book can prove useful. The aim of this book is to deepen and clarify INTPs' understanding of their personality (Part I), their purpose (Part II), and their philosophy (Part III), as well as their path to integration and the successful enactment of their purpose (Part IV).

More specifically, Part I (Chapters 1-4) explores each of INTPs' four personality functions (i.e., Ti, Ne, Si, and Fe), as well as their implications for the INTP quest. The operating assumption of these chapters is that personality type plays a foundational role in shaping and informing their purpose. So if INTPs can learn more about their personality and the various tools in their cognitive toolbox, they can better understand who they are and the sorts of things they might do with those tools.

Part II (Chapters 5-7) considers what INTPs are seeking in a purpose. Chapter 5 explores two key elements of purpose, importance and energy, while Chapter 6 examines the critical role of ideas and concepts in INTPs' quest for purpose. Chapter 7 looks at INTPs' struggle to balance the introverted (I) and extraverted (E) factors in their purpose equation, such as their attempt to reconcile their need to authentically follow their own (often esoteric) interests (I) with their desire for recognition and a respectable income (E).

Part III (Chapters 8-13) takes a closer look at INTPs' philosophical propensities, including the types of concepts, philosophers, and philosophies they may be drawn to. It includes discussions of religion, theism vs. atheism vs. pantheism, mind and matter, free will and determinism, history, existentialism, and more. The purpose of these discussions is to explore how INTPs think, and the types of ideas and thinkers to which they gravitate. This can help INTPs see where they fit into the larger world of ideas, as well as better understand and embrace their natural philosophical inclinations. By clarifying who they are as thinkers, INTPs will find it easier to envision their optimal place in the world.

Finally, Part IV (Chapter 14-16) explores issues that will be of particular interest to INTPs who are further along in their quest. Chapter 14 examines INTPs' concerns regarding shortages of novelty and meaning as they approach the end of their seeker's quest. Chapter 15 discusses the sense of deflation that can accompany the loss of ideals over time, including the challenges associated with the discovery of one's purpose. Chapter 16 seeks a remedy for the problems introduced in Chapter 15. Namely, it explores how INTPs can effectively navigate what I call the "post-idealist" phase of life through the adoption of a certain type of mindset. Not only can this mindset assuage INTPs' foremost existential concerns, but it can also help them effectively enact their purpose and experience integration.

Notes

1. Following what has become a conventional practice among typologists, that of declaring one's own type, I hereby announce that I am an INTP.

2. If type operates outside of conscious awareness, then how was it discovered and explicated? Typologists do so largely by observing patterns of similarity (and difference) *across* individuals. In other words, they employ what amounts to a sociological approach. This is essentially what Jung claimed to have done in deriving his typological framework from years of observations with his psychiatric clientele.

3. Readers who are new to typology are encouraged to explore my earlier work, *My True Type*, or visit my blog, personalityjunkie.com, to acquire additional background information. While newcomers to type can still benefit from this book, it is assumed that readers possess at least a baseline understanding of certain type basics. Readers are also encouraged to consult my prior book, *The INTP*, for an in-depth description and analysis of the INTP personality type.

PART I

The INTP Personality

1

INTRODUCED THINKING (TI)

Each personality type uses four functions that comprise its functional stack. The functions are ordered according to their relative degree of strength and development, as well as their availability for conscious employment. The most developed and conscious function is the dominant function, followed by the auxiliary, tertiary, and inferior functions respectively.

INTPs' functional stack is as follows:

Dominant function: Introverted Thinking (Ti)

Auxiliary function: Extraverted Intuition (Ne)

Tertiary function: Introverted Sensing (Si)

Inferior function: Extraverted Feeling (Fe)

In working to understand the foundations of INTPs' personality type, not to mention their life's purpose, Introverted Thinking (Ti) is a good place to start. As INTPs' dominant function, Ti is in many respects the captain of their psychological ship. It is their default or "first option" for navigating life.

In order to grasp the essential nature of Ti, it can be helpful to compare and contrast it with its thinking counterpart, Extraverted Thinking (Te). Te orients its reasoning to collective standards and procedures, as well as empirical and quantitative data. Whenever possible, its data is collected under tightly controlled circumstances (e.g., controlled experiments) in order to precisely measure the effects of manipulating a single variable. Science is a quintessential embodiment of Te, as evidenced in its heavy reliance on formal experimentation, measurement, quantification, and standardized methods.

The workings of Ti are more informal, holistic, qualitative, and impromptu. Typologist Lenore Thomson suggests that Ti predominates in tasks requiring situational logic, such as aligning and hammering a nail. In determining where and how to strike a nail, Ti uses a technique colloquially known as "eyeballing," that is, it quickly and informally appraises the situation (e.g., the size of the hammer, length of the nail, thickness of the board, etc.), making adjustments as necessary with each successive strike. If we compare this with the amount of forethought and preparation required for a scientific experiment, we get a snapshot of some of the core Te-Ti differences.

As an introverted function, Ti relies on its own inner logic and manufactures its own ways of doing things. In many respects, this makes Ti a more portable and versatile function. Instead of referencing external protocols and "doing things by the book" (Te), Ti is confident in its ability to spontaneously and independently figure things out. Characteristically clever and innovative, Ti can engineer hacks or workarounds in nearly any situation.

Holistic Essences

While Ti is undoubtedly useful for navigating the concrete world and solving practical challenges, it can also be applied conceptually and theoretically, especially when coupled with INTPs' auxiliary function, Ne. It is largely Ti that compels INTPs to understand the *essence of things*, including their essential self, purpose, and philosophy.[1] While all the judging functions (i.e., Ti, Fi, Te, and Fe) work to establish firm beliefs, methods, or values, because Ti is both an introverted and a thinking function, it is particularly concerned with those that are essential or foundational. Te, by contrast, is more fact-oriented and therefore more comfortable with pluralities (as opposed to singularities or essences). In this sense, Ti is more reductive than Te. It attempts to strip away particulars and boil down pluralities so that only what is essential or foundational remains. In mathematical parlance, Ti is constantly seeking the "lowest common denominator."

While Ti can be seen as acting reductively in its quest for foundational knowledge, it is actually more *holistic* in its approach than Te is. Te strives to reduce or eliminate the subjective contributions of the investigator in order to allow "the facts to speak for themselves." Such an approach is characteristic of what we know about the left side of the brain, which is why Te is considered a "left-brained" function. Conversely, Ti trusts and embraces its own subjectivity, considering it a useful and necessary tool for discerning truth, and especially wisdom. Unlike Te, Ti incorporates information from both sides of the brain. Its right-brained element imbues it with a softness, roundness, and openness that is lacking in the Te approach. It also brings more nuance to the Ti perspective, seeing things in shades of grey rather than black and white.

Autonomous, Serious, & Work-Oriented

Insistent on marching to the beat of their own drummer, INTPs are the most fiercely independent of all types. Leading with Ti, they are self-directed and self-taught. They follow their own lead with little need for external aids or prompts. Because their autonomy is so central to who they are, they are very protective of their time and freedom. They can become frustrated or resentful when others try to coerce or make demands of them. They instinctively resist, even if mostly inwardly, actual or perceived threats to their autonomy. Consequently, INTPs aren't always the best team players. While they may go with the flow for a while, they eventually get restless and want to work independently. For it is only when they are alone, or are otherwise granted ample freedom, that they feel most themselves.

As a judging function, Ti is inclined to take life rather seriously. While some personality types see having fun as their primary life objective, INTPs want more from life than just fun and games. Like ISTPs, they bring a characteristically work-oriented approach to life. They seek a central purpose in which they can consistently invest their time, thought, and energy.

Independent Judging & Filtering

As an introverted judging function, Ti prefers to make its own independent assessments and utilize its own evaluative criteria, the validity of which are experienced as self-evident. It is relatively unconcerned with whether others agree with its methods or conclusions. The independent and self-referencing nature of Ti has largely contributed to INTPs' reputation as armchair philosophers. According to Jung:

> "The introverted thinking type is strongly influenced by ideas, though his ideas have their origin not in objective data but in his subjective foundation . . . However clear to him the inner structure of his thoughts may be, he is not the least clear where or how they link up with reality."[2]

Not only does Ti feel perfectly at home making its own judgments, but it also serves as a filter for incoming information. If something is perceived as irrelevant to its current objectives, Ti will ignore or dismiss it. Due to this filtering propensity, INTPs can be subject to developing tunnel vision. As Jung observed:

> "With the intensification of his type, his convictions become all the more rigid and unbending. Outside influences are shut off; as a person, too, he becomes more unsympathetic to his wider circle of acquaintances . . . Because of the

subjectivization of consciousness . . . what secretly concerns his own person now seems to him of extreme importance."[3]

While it is true that INTPs in some respects "live in their own subjective world," most are not pure isolationists. Their Ne and Fe functions serve to counterbalance Ti, prompting INTPs to periodically look beyond themselves and consider outside information.

Summary of Ti Characteristics

- Can operate concretely or conceptually
- Works to discern underlying essences through nuanced and holistic logic
- Takes a serious, work-oriented approach to life
- Prefers to work independently and autonomously; values self-direction
- Develops its own methods and strategies
- Evaluates / filters incoming information to ensure relevance and usefulness
- Potential interests: Independent or self-directed projects of all sorts; activities involving analysis, strategy, problem-solving, or critical thinking

Notes

1. It is interesting to note that, despite using the same four functions as INTPs (albeit in a different order), ENTPs are rarely as obsessed with nailing down their identity to the degree that INTPs are. This is because ENTPs use Ne as their dominant function, which is less concerned with ideational essences and consolidation than Ti is.

2. Jung, CG. *Psychological Types*. Para. 632-634.

3. Jung, CG. *Psychological Types*. Para. 636.

2
EXTRAVERTED INTUITION (NE)

"If I were to wish for anything, I should not wish for wealth and power, but for the passionate sense of the potential . . . for the eye which sees the possible. Pleasure disappoints, possibility never."

—*Kierkegaard, Either / Or*

When considered independently, Ti is not necessarily abstract or theoretical. It is not until it teams up with its auxiliary sidekick, Extraverted Intuition (Ne), that INTPs' thinking becomes more characteristically abstract, conceptual, or philosophical.

As enumerated in *The 16 Personality Types*, the development of the functions generally occurs from the top of the functional stack downward (i.e., Ti then Ne, etc). Because Ne is the second function in their developmental sequence, young INTPs, in particular, may be relatively unaware of their ideational (i.e., N) propensities (especially if their parents are both S types). While their Ne is always operating in the background, it takes time for INTPs to develop an explicit or consistent interest in the world of ideas. Indeed, INTPs may be well into their twenties before becoming fully immersed in Ne explorations. This is important because INTPs who have yet to intently explore Ne matters will see the world, and their purpose, quite differently from those who have. Imagine the difference, for instance, between the life of an INTP before discovering their love of theology or philosophy, versus how it might look after. For many INTPs, the difference is like night and day.

INTPs who have yet to develop Ne may also think and behave more conventionally. They may focus on their schooling and relationships, without thinking too deeply about the bigger picture of things. Only when they open themselves to the world of Ne ideas and possibilities do they become full-blown seekers. And once Ne takes center stage, their quest for purpose becomes exceedingly more complex. While adulthood complicates matters for all types, Ne can make things worse, augmenting any sense of confusion, indecision, or restlessness. Here is a quick overview of the reasons for this:

- Ne perpetually pushes for the pursuit of novelty. This engenders a sense of restlessness and makes it difficult for INTPs to make long-term commitments or investments.

- Ne multiplies the number of ideas, options, and possibilities INTPs must contend with. Seeing multiple sides of, or myriad options for nearly everything, decision-making is rendered increasingly difficult.

- Ne introduces a philosophical element into INTPs' purpose seeking. This means their purpose must not only entail plenty of autonomy and independence (Ti), but must also incorporate their philosophical (or religious) interests and worldview.

Openness to Novelty & Exploration

Ne is similar to its sensing cousin, Extraverted Sensation (Se), in that both are concerned with the open-ended pursuit of novelty. The difference of course is that Se is oriented toward sensory novelty— new sights, sounds, tastes, etc.—whereas Ne is fascinated by new ideas, connections, and possibilities. This distinction was highlighted in our earlier quote from Kierkegaard, "Pleasure (Se) disappoints, possibility (Ne) never."

Ne strongly and positively correlates with the Big Five personality domain called *openness to experience* (a.k.a., *openness*), which includes openness to ideas, values, feelings, actions, and aesthetics. While INTPs' degree of openness may vary according to time and circumstance, they typically score relatively high on the openness scale (although usually less than ENPs, who use Ne as their dominant function).

Studies suggest that openness is also positively correlated with global levels of the neurotransmitter, dopamine, which personality researcher Colin DeYoung has dubbed the "neuromodulator of exploration."[1] DeYoung defines exploration as "any behavior or cognition motivated by the incentive reward value of uncertainty." He suggests that individuals with open and explorative minds also exhibit higher levels of "psychological entropy," with entropy referring to the "uncertainty or unpredictability" of a given system.

In light of DeYoung's work, we might conclude that INTPs, even if unwittingly, keep themselves open to novelty (Ne) because doing so positively affects their dopamine levels. And while there is some measure of risk and uncertainty (i.e., entropy / instability) associated with novel explorations, the anticipated psychological payoff may be too alluring to resist. Although younger INTPs may seek novelty through things like sports, drugs, or sex, more seasoned INTPs typically turn to the world of ideas to satisfy their explorational needs.

Connecting, Synthesizing, & Creating

Ne is constantly making associations and seeing parallels, even among what other personality types might consider disparate or unrelated ideas. This is why conversations between two NPs are typically broad-ranging, as one idea or association begets another, *ad infinitum*. This also explains why INTPs are drawn to interdisciplinary studies. They love exploring the parallels of different subjects, seeing how the conceptual patterns of one discipline resemble or connect with those of another. One can witness the effects of Ne in the works of INTP writers, theorists, artists, and inventors, all of whom rely on Ne's penchant for discovering new associations, syntheses, or applications.

In constantly making new connections, Ne can multiply ideas or possibilities at a rapid rate. In this respect, it is almost synonymous with divergent thinking, which *Wikipedia* defines as "a thought process or method used to generate creative ideas by exploring many possible solutions." While divergent thinking can be used intentionally, as this definition implies, it commonly occurs spontaneously (e.g., "The idea just came to me."), especially in NP types. Considering the characteristically creative nature of Ne, INTPs are right to see themselves as one of the more creative personality types.[2]

I contend that most INTPs who have successfully found their purpose would attest to the importance of creativity in their work. This would even hold true for INTP businessmen like Bill Gates. Not only did Gates rely on creative thought in the development of his products, but also in formulating strategies and envisioning new enterprises for his company.

Doubt & Uncertainty

As we've seen, Ne is associated with the open-ended exploration of ideas and possibilities. This can be exhilarating for INTPs, providing plenty of "food for thought" and a healthy dose of dopamine to boot. At the same time, Ne can introduce ample doubt and uncertainty (or to use DeYoung's term, entropy), as well as anxiety, into the INTP's world.

In their younger years, the INTP's world may feel rather safe and small, conferring a sense of comfort and protection. But with the advent of adulthood and the flowering of their Ne, INTPs may suddenly find themselves facing a vast sea of ideas and possibilities. This can be overwhelming for INTPs, who may feel ill-equipped to process such a glut of options. It can prove especially unsettling for Ti, which demands a certain measure of order and certainty in the INTP's worldview.

In addition to exponentially expanding the number of ideas and options they feel compelled to explore, Ne also makes it difficult for INTPs to make firm judgments about what they believe. INTPs have a propensity for doubt and vacillation. They may feel excited and confident about an idea one day, only to feel ambivalent about it the next. They can quickly transition from a blissful sense of having THE answer to the dreadful feeling that they know nothing at all.

INTPs' indecisiveness is not limited to their identity and purpose, but also affects their careers and relationships. This is due in large part to their desire to clarify their identity prior to committing to a career or relationship. As long as their sense of self remains muddled or uncertain, they may feel incapable of authentically committing to much of anything.

In response to the myriad challenges presented by adulthood and the flowering of their Ne, INTPs may try to simplify things by focusing primarily on clarifying their identity, perhaps telling themselves they'll worry about everything else later. But once they've plunged themselves deep into Ne, how can they clarify their identity without also clarifying their worldview? Even if they prioritize the clarification of their self-concept, their identity must, at least to some extent, be informed by an understanding of the world and its extant ideas. INTPs are therefore left with little choice but to acknowledge the enormity of the task before them. Not only must they know themselves, but they must also understand the larger drama of life, humanity, and the cosmos in order to see how everything fits together in a coherent and unified way.

Summary of Ne Characteristics

- Associated with a need for novelty and exploration
- Generates new ideas, associations, connections, and possibilities
- Pushes for exploration, creativity, and innovation
- Wants to "keep options open"; resists commitment to a single path or idea
- Contributes to doubt, indecision, and uncertainty
- Can have a philosophical, mystical, or spiritual quality
- Potential interests: Any activity involving creative, explorative, or theoretical ideation

Notes

1. DeYoung, C.G. The Neuromodulator of Exploration: A Unifying Theory of the Role of Dopamine in Personality. *Frontiers of Human Neuroscience.* 2013.

2. According to the *MBTI Manual*, creativity correlates most strongly with the N preference, as well as, to a lesser extent, the P preference. Thus, NPs tend to be the most creative of all types.

3
INTROVERTED SENSING (SI)

"Life can only be understood backwards."

—Kierkegaard

As we saw in the previous chapter, INTPs often struggle to draw firm conclusions or make enduring commitments. This can be discouraging and frustrating, perhaps even causing them to wonder if they will ever manage to pin down their purpose. It is therefore fortunate that their tertiary Si, if properly employed, can help move them toward greater certainty in their beliefs and understanding.

In *My True Type*, I associate Si with "learning through experience." For instance, we discover at an early age that touching a hot stove is painful; it only takes one bad experience to learn this valuable life lesson. Despite the apparent simplicity of this example, it clearly demonstrates how experience (S) can translate into knowledge.

With that said, when we consider the hierarchical ordering of INTPs' functional stack, we discover that sensory / empirical / experiential evidence, which we can roughly associate with Si (or sensing generally), is typically of lower priority than insights provided through reason (Ti) or intuition (Ne). From this we can deduce that experience, especially on its own, doesn't always constitute knowledge for INTPs.

While in no way denying the real danger presented by things like hot stoves, an INTP might make the general point that experience is not always reliable or trustworthy. Phenomena such as optical illusions and hallucinations may be cited as examples. And because S perceptions are not always reliable, they must be evaluated, typically by Ti, to confirm (or reject) their validity, utility, or value. In other cases, INTPs may merely ignore, even unwittingly, S facts or details, which seem too banal or trivial to warrant their Ti or Ne concern. In philosophical parlance, INTPs are rationalists before they are empiricists. They are wired to prioritize reason over experience or empirical data.

With that said, INTPs will nonetheless benefit from incorporating some measure of life experience or empirical data into their worldview. Doing so can provide them with a sense of confidence and certainty that may be lacking if relying solely on Ti and Ne. Unfortunately, INTPs can be rather impatient when it comes to sifting through S information. Their preference is to extract the main points, to "get the gist," without getting bogged down in S details.

Another of INTPs' hesitations with respect to incorporating S information involves determining the reliability of a given piece of evidence. Without engaging in a thorough background investigation (which INTPs are loathe to do), how can its validity be confirmed? While other types may turn to consensus (Fe) or established authorities (Te), these sources may fail to convince the more skeptical INTP. Perhaps the bigger question is this: Who or what can INTPs trust beyond their own reasoning?

INTPs seem more apt to trust evidence that is less easily manipulated by other human beings. This may include certain types of scientific or historic evidence, as well as evidence delivered directly through their own senses or personal experience. While INTPs always enlist Ti to scrutinize their personal experiences, they tend to trust their own experiences and observations more than the testimonies of others.[1,2]

The Maze Metaphor

In hopes of clarifying their foundational understanding, INTPs can recall their past experiences with Si, use Ne to discern patterns among those experiences, and employ Ti to check for logical soundness and potential utility. To further illustrate this process, we will now turn to "the maze metaphor," which was conceived a few years ago by my typology sidekick, Elaine Schallock.

Schallock suggests that the INTP's process of understanding resembles that of navigating a hedge or corn maze. The participants in a hedge maze do not enjoy the advantage of a bird's eye view (as would be the case with a maze printed on paper) because of its tall and opaque surrounding walls. Rather, participants (in this case, INTPs) can only see the paths in their immediate purview. Thus, in order to complete the maze, INTPs are forced to explore myriad paths (Ne), most of which will turn out to be dead-ends. They must also recall (Si) which paths were dead-ends in order to avoid retreading old ground.

The maze metaphor illustrates how INTPs use trial-and-error and knowledge of past experiences (Si) to help them clarify their understanding and direction in life. With time and experimentation, INTPs gradually develop more confidence and certainty in their beliefs and identity.[3]

Surveying Past Beliefs & Experiences

One reason finding purpose in the modern world can be so difficult is we've lost our ability to know what we, as individuals, really believe. In part, this stems from the presence of so many competing voices, ideas, and possibilities in our heads. Like other types, INTPs can also fall prey to believing that the loudest or most celebrated voices, such as those of prominent public intellectuals, are the correct or optimal ones. While surveying circulating ideas (Ne) can help INTPs key-in to the types of ideas that resonate with them, they need to ensure that it is their own self that is given the final say in their beliefs.

During my twenties and early thirties, I experienced a lengthy period of ambivalence regarding my own beliefs. I prided myself in my ability to see both sides of every issue and to eschew strong opinions; I was the king of neutral. One might say I was functioning as a good pluralist, relativist, or postmodernist. But in all honesty, I wasn't all that happy as a neutralist, but longed to discover something I really believed in, something that could imbue my life with purpose and direction. At some point, I felt it imperative to identify the beliefs that came naturally to me, those that emerged straight from my core self. I suspected that my innate ideational propensities might have been buried or masked by my explorations of outside ideas; I feared that all my reading may have been obscuring, rather than clarifying, my true self. If the self was to serve as the foundation of my purpose, it was time that I work to understand its natural propensities apart from outside influence.

So like any good INTP, I decided to conduct a thought experiment, or perhaps more accurately, an Si experiment, in which I would inventory my past beliefs. I suspected that doing so might reveal recurring patterns in my thought, something more trustworthy than whatever my "idea of the day" (Ne) happened to be. In other words, I was curious to see if Si could offer me a measure of clarity and conviction that Ne seemed incapable of providing. Frankly, the prospect of conducting this exercise was a bit nerve-racking since a lot seemed to be riding on it. What if I came up empty? What if my entire intellectual journey had been futile, producing nothing in the way of real answers or convictions? That was a terrifying, yet real possibility. Nevertheless, I put these hesitations aside and carried out the experiment. I decided to make two lists, one containing my historical self-related beliefs and the other my world-related beliefs. Much to my delight (and relief), the experiment was a success. There before me was a rather lengthy account of things I had come to believe about myself and the world. In reviewing the lists, I saw evidence of two things I had hoped to find: evidence that I was naturally inclined toward certain beliefs and ways of knowing, and evidence that I had in fact made progress in clarifying my beliefs. I was also surprised by the deep sense of pleasure and resonance I experienced in revisiting my past beliefs. It was similar to the feeling one gets when encountering a likeminded thinker or a "kindred spirit," the sense that "this person really gets it!" Only in this case, I was essentially resonating with my past self. Moreover, I was pleased to discover that many of my ideational propensities had remained largely unchanged, even over a decade later. This consistency reassured me that clarifying my identity and purpose was a real possibility.

This is not to say that retrospection will always yield a singular inner voice. Especially early in the process, it may be difficult to disentangle one's own voice from those of others. Individuals with more life experience may enjoy some advantage in this respect, since they will have accumulated more data from which to extract patterns. For it is the recurring, deeply engrained patterns—those emerging from the core self—that INTPs are most concerned with.

From Dilettante (Ne) to Expert (Si)

While INTPs rarely display the same breadth of interests as ENPs, Ne can still make it hard for them to pin down their niche interest. Ne can be restless and impatient, causing INTPs to worry that they will never stick with anything long enough to become an expert. They may conclude that becoming a specialist requires too much sustained focus or attention to detail.

We typically think of experts as having specific Te credentials, such as specialized degrees or certifications. But for INTPs, an area of expertise often does not pre-exist "out there." There is no perfect pre-fab job or career program for INTPs. Rather, their area of expertise is a unique synthesis of their personal interests. Because it is unique to them, they are responsible for discovering and cultivating it. The world cannot give them expertise in the form of a degree. Rather, INTPs must discover their own niche, however idiosyncratic, and bring it to the world.

Even Kant (an INTP) was a late bloomer with respect to finding his primary niche. Kant didn't publish his masterpiece, *Critique of Pure Reason*, until well into his fifties. The same can be said of the INTP writer Robert Pirsig, whose classic work, *Zen and the Art of Motorcycle Maintenance*, didn't hit the shelves until he was in his forties. This is consistent with Jung's observation of the introverted thinker: "His work goes slowly and with difficulty."

The Value of Si for William James

The famous American philosopher and scientist, William James, is a great case study for illustrating the value of developing and integrating Si for an NP type.[4] Early in life, James desperately struggled to discern his purpose in life, being riddled with Ne doubt and uncertainty. He even suffered a rather protracted period of severe depression and psychological instability. There seemed to be too many life paths before him and he couldn't decide which was right for him. Fortunately, James managed to see his way out of this debacle. And most important for our purposes, he described his road to salvation in characteristically Si terms.

For one, James came to herald the value of developing habits. If you know much about Si dominants (i.e., ISFJs and ISTJs), you'll know that they are creatures of habit. And while James was clearly an NP type, he found that habits in many ways saved him from the constant indecision and vacillations of Ne. In *Habit*, James penned:

> "The more of the details of our daily life we can hand over to the effortless custody of automatism, the more our higher powers of mind will be set free for their own proper work.

There is no more miserable human being than one in whom nothing is habitual but indecision, and for whom the lighting of every cigar, the drinking of every cup, the time of rising and going to bed every day, and the beginning of every bit of work, are subjects of express volitional deliberation."

The value of Si for William James was also evidenced in his commitment to his work and his development of scientific and philosophic expertise. But even then, James was not just a physician-scientist. As an NP, his interests remained synthetic. He seemed to find his niche at the crossroads of psychology and philosophy, seasoned with a pinch of religion and spirituality.

In sum, James' development of effective habits and his committed investment in specific interest areas allowed him to overcome his earlier state of Ne paralysis. His successful integration of Si granted him a clearer sense of purpose and helped him become one of America's most celebrated intellectuals.

Final Thoughts

As discussed in *My True Type*, the shape associated with INTPs' (and other IPs') functional stack is that of a diamond. It starts with a Ti point of focus, broadens outward with Ne, then starts to converge again with Si and Fe. This diamond pattern is also illustrative of INTPs' process of type development.

As suggested by the maze metaphor, Ne must be allowed to do its thing, to explore myriad possibilities, before INTPs can move forward with confidence. But as they explore more options over time—more routes in the maze—and recall what they've already experienced (Si), they gain a clearer sense of the overall picture, including the nature of their core interests. This corresponds with the developmental trajectory of their functional stack, moving from Ne breadth toward greater Si convergence.

Incorporating Si evidence can help INTPs feel more confident about who they are and what they believe. Equally important, it can keep them from becoming cynical toward the prospect of greater certainty. While they may trust some types of evidence more than others, this is still better than feeling there is nothing they can trust at all.

As INTPs mature and feel more confident in themselves and their purpose, they become a bit more patient with, and appreciative of, certain Si details. Instead of Ne being so domineering, their Ne and Si start to work more as a team.

Developing Si may also engender a sense of calm and assurance in INTPs. When sufficient Si data has been incorporated into their cognitive process, it is no longer necessary for INTPs to seek far and wide (Ne) for their purpose because their Si can remind them of its general vicinity. While their purpose may always remain somewhat fluid and versatile, Si can at least make it solid enough to not slip through their fingers.

Summary of Si Characteristics

- Retains, consolidates, and recollects information acquired through life experience
- Uses evidence or past experience to inform thinking and decision-making
- Associated with habits and commitment
- Attentive to concrete details and specifics
- Potential interest areas: Anything related to one's personal past or our collective past (e.g., history, archeology)

Notes

1. This is one way INTPs differ from INTJs. INTJs generally place more trust in recognized authorities or collectively established methodologies (Te).

They seem more apt to criticize personal experience as anecdotal, which the scientific community has deemed an invalid form of evidence. INTPs are, in some respects, the opposite. Since they don't fully trust scientific investigators or their methods (especially in the soft or applied sciences), they don't put science on a pedestal in the way INTJs are inclined to do. Instead, INTPs place more trust in their own reasoning (Ti), as well as, to some extent, their own life experiences (Si). INTPs may also borrow or springboard off of others' ideas (Ne), but they rarely accept them uncritically. Since INTJs' Te is less critical in its workings than Ti (similar to how Fe is less critical than Fi), they seem more disposed to accept scientific or other authoritative claims as hard truths than INTPs are.

2. Personal experience proved to be a critical factor in substantiating my belief and confidence in Jungian typology. When first introduced to Jung's thought, I was skeptical of the functions, which seemed too ideal or contrived to possibly be real. What forced me to reconsider my position was my exposure to a long string of INTJ-INTP interactions. I was at once amazed and perplexed by how two of the most brilliant personality types repeatedly and vehemently disagreed about what constituted truth (those of you who have participated in personality forums may have experienced something similar in your interactions with INTJs). It seemed to me that whenever INTJs wanted to use intuition, INTPs would respond with a logic-based objection (Ti). Similarly, whenever INTPs preferred to lead with intuition, INTJs would counter with scientific facts or argumentation (Te). Simply put, these two types, while similar in many respects, seemed to consistently fail to see eye-to-eye. After seeing these patterns of confrontation repeat themselves over and over, I was forced to conclude that there must be profound psychological differences between these two types, something that extended beyond mere J-P differences. I eventually conceded that it was only through the lens of the functions (and the functional stack) that these differences could be made sensible.

3. We might contrast INTPs' experimental maze-solving approach with the approach taken by INJ types. According to Schallock, INJs enjoy readier access to the bird's eye view because of their dominant Ni. Since Ni is a perceiving function, she contends that INJs perceive more information on the front end than INTPs, which may privy them to a more comprehensive view of things. This ostensibly keeps INJs from having to personally trial every possible route in the maze. As we saw in Chapter 1, leading with Ti can give INTPs a sort of tunnel vision, seeing only what Ti expects or wants to see. This is consistent with Schallock's point about INJs perceiving more on the front end.

Another pertinent consideration is Ni, as an introverted perceiving function, tends to see a single coherent picture of things and INJs trust the accuracy of that picture. This is why INJs typically don't see themselves as *seekers*, but rather as *knowers*. Ne, by contrast, sees multiple possibilities and struggles to know, especially on its own, which one is correct or optimal. So it's not that INTPs don't strive to acquire a bird's eye view. The problem is determining which view is the correct one. An INJ might argue that INTPs aren't zooming out far enough to allow a clearer view of things to emerge. Hence, what INTPs believe to be a bird's eye view may in fact capture only part of the maze. This is why experience / evidence is important for INTPs. It reminds them that they have explored all the necessary options and are therefore accurately seeing the bigger picture.

4. Unfortunately, all I can say with certainty about James' type is that he was an NP. If forced to venture a guess, I would go with ENTP. The degree to which he seemed to see Si as a panacea suggests it was likely his inferior function. Moreover, I don't see James emphasizing philosophical foundations in the way I would expect to see from an INTP. I do however see him as a kindred spirit, which is often the case between INTPs and ENTPs.

4

EXTRAVERTED FEELING (FE)

Extraverted Feeling (Fe) is INTPs' inferior function. Because the inferior function operates largely on an unconscious level, all types struggle to grasp and understand its essential nature. It represents a sort of strange and foreign land, one which is poorly understood. For this reason, it is sometimes described as the lost, missing, or repressed function. In dreams, it may be symbolized as something deep underground, undersea, or in a dark forest.

Despite its relative unconsciousness, the psychospiritual importance of the inferior function cannot be downplayed or ignored. It plays a surprisingly powerful role in the motivations and developmental trajectory of each personality type. There are a number of reasons it has more psychological influence than we might initially expect.

First, the inferior function is inextricably linked with the dominant function. As functional opposites, they exist in a perpetual state of tension and dialogue with each other; whatever one function does invariably affects the other. So if INTPs' Ti becomes too extreme or domineering, Fe will rebel and demand more attention. The reverse is also true.

Second, the inferior function is typically perceived as refreshingly new and novel. Engendering experiences characteristically distinct from those of the dominant, it can feel magical and mysterious, even blissful. It is therefore no surprise that all personality types feel compelled to explore and understand their inferior function.

Finally, the inferior is the last function to be developed and integrated in the functional stack. It therefore represents a sort of pinnacle of type development, the last leg of the quest for wholeness. Combine this with its poignant sense of magic and mystery, and the inferior may seem nothing less than godlike, the key to our salvation. All that is needed, then, is a reliable way of accessing, harnessing, and integrating it.

Such is the vantage point from which all types start their development. They feel that something critical is missing from their lives (e.g. the inferior function) and their purpose is to find that Holy Grail so they can experience life in all of its fullness.

INTPs' "Missing Function"

As we've seen, INTPs are generally comfortable and competent with thinking and intuition, and to some extent, with sensing. But feeling is another story. Like other types, INTPs sense that one of their functions is somehow "lost" or "missing" because of its distinctive unconsciousness. Their missing / inferior function is Extraverted Feeling (Fe), which they experience as slippery, elusive, and outside their conscious control. Hence, when it comes to knowing how they feel about things (as opposed to what they think), INTPs are largely in the dark.[1]

Compared to other types (especially F types), INTPs often lack strong feelings of love (i.e., deep feeling attachments to other people), empathy, or compassion. Even in tragic situations, such as upon hearing news of a terrorist attack or natural disaster, they may *feel* relatively little. Whatever empathy they have stems mostly from cognitive rather than affective sources. As much as INTPs might want to experience or express genuine empathy, the feelings simply aren't there; there is little for them to work with.

It's not that INTPs never experience feelings, or even strong feelings. In fact, there are certain types of situations (e.g., romantic infatuation), music (e.g., love songs), films (e.g., dramas), or memories (e.g., childhood) that will reliably stir up emotion or sentimentalism in INTPs, even to the point of tears. INTPs also have a somewhat reliable, even if nebulous, sense of their overall mood, such as whether they feel restless, irritable, anxious, or excited.

Curiously, INTPs seem to have readier access to, or more familiarity with, strong negative emotions than they do positive ones. When around certain people or in certain situations, strong feelings of anger, disgust, or hostility may occasionally erupt into their consciousness, seemingly out of nowhere (see *The INTP* for more on this). Unfortunately, INTPs often fail to experience commensurate levels of positive emotions, excepting romantic infatuation or instances when they artificially stoke their emotions.

Idealizing the Inferior Function

As we've seen, the inferior function is commonly experienced as magical and mysterious, having almost a divine quality to it. And because INTPs' inferior function is feeling, they are inclined to venerate F ideals such as meaning, value, significance, and importance.

Dominant feeling types, by contrast, are inclined to emphasize T ideals. INFPs, for instance, commonly emphasize the importance of truth (T) in their lives. Consider the following quotes from my INFP friend's blog: "I just want the world to make sense . . . I use the intellect to justify my existence . . . I worship at the altar of truth . . . Truth is my religion . . . I want truth to matter to other people."[2]

If we were to substitute the word meaning (or purpose) for truth in the above statements, we would get a good sense of the INTP's perspective:

"I just want the world to be meaningful . . . I use meaning to justify my existence . . . I worship at the altar of meaning . . . Meaning is my religion . . . I want meaning to matter to other people."[3]

This is what makes the inferior function fascinating, not to mention tricky and misleading. It constantly orchestrates these sorts of inversions, so that what we would expect to see from one type (e.g., a thinker venerating T things) actually manifests in another (e.g., a feeler venerating T things). No wonder so many people experience type confusion!

Energy, Motivation, & the Inferior Function

Both Jung and Freud saw the human psyche as possessing its own type of energy, which they referred to as *libido*. Both viewed the conscious mind as rather impotent in its ability to generate libido, instead seeing the unconscious as the primary storehouse or wellspring of libido.

If it is true that the unconscious serves as our main source of libido and that the inferior function operates unconsciously, it does not seem unreasonable to suspect that the inferior function might play role in regulating libido. And this is precisely what we find. All types naturally come to associate their inferior function with energy and motivation, which is why they typically grant it inordinate amounts of attention and interest. It seems to operate as a sort of portal or supply line to a well of unconscious energy.

In some of my past writings, I have emphasized (perhaps over-emphasized) the potential downsides of being led or motivated by the inferior function. A common argument against leading with the inferior function goes something like this: "T types should not be focusing on F matters because this constitutes a poor use of their typological strengths. They are better off working on T matters, leaving the F work to the F types." Logically, this argument makes a good deal of sense. In a perfect world, we might want T types working in science and technology and F types handling moral and social issues. But the proverbial elephant in the room is motivation. Namely, if people don't feel inspired in their work, then how well will they actually perform? Put differently, to what extent can motivation, and the persistence it inspires, compensate for deficits in natural talent?

It may be that nature, in wiring us to focus on the inferior function, has failed with respect to optimizing our performance as individuals. But one could also argue that ignoring the inferior function poses an even greater danger. What would happen, for instance, if thinkers were completely devoid of F concerns? Is this not what we see with psychopaths? Perhaps our intrigue with the inferior helps ensure some basic level of competence with all the functions? Maybe it is more important for us to be somewhat balanced than extraordinarily good at one thing.

All in all, I fear that I've underemphasized the importance and value of the inferior function as a source of energy and motivation. If we care about purpose and vitality, we may have little choice but to grant it a seat at the table.

Potential Paths for Integrating Fe

Wittingly or not, INTPs take up the quest to discover and integrate their inferior Fe. The ways in which they do so will vary according to circumstances, as well as their respective stage of type development.

At some point in childhood, INTPs discover that they can stoke their feelings through certain types of music, movies, books, or fantasies. This, combined with the dream of one day finding their ideal love, may energize them for many years. Young INTPs may also set their sights on broad-scale affirmation and recognition. They may dream of becoming famous in hopes of securing an infinite supply of Fe praise and adulation. But as enumerated in *The INTP*, these dreams often crumble when INTPs discover that their long-anticipated ideals were illusory, nothing but a mirage engineered by their inferior function.

Once it becomes clear that INTPs' childhood fantasies were illusory or unrealistic, they start looking for new ways of integrating their Fe. Developmentally, this often coincides with the development of Ne (i.e., Phase II of type development[4]). Hence, their new approach will typically have a strong N component. They may, for instance, aspire to become a sage.[5] Having awakened their N powers, they may set their sights on solving the riddles of the human condition (Fe). And while pursuing sagehood is a more mature enterprise for INTPs than chasing romantic ideals, it is not without its difficulties. For one, the role of a sage involves issuing firm F answers, advice, and guidance. But because INTPs' Fe is so unconscious and inaccessible, they often feel ill-equipped to proffer firm advice. They may feel perfectly comfortable telling you how to fix your computer (T), but not your emotional struggles or your relationships (F). INTPs who do offer F answers, often do so in a type-biased way, such as promoting strategies that come natural to Ti (i.e., emotional detachment, cognitive reframing, etc.) but may ultimately prove less beneficial to other types.

Another way INTPs may try to integrate their Fe is through engaging with others. They may, for instance, dabble in various discussion or interest groups, sensing that this may help them marry their Ti, Ne, and Fe. INTPs enjoy talking about ideas, especially those that matter to them. It is rarely long, however, before their social interest wanes or they start feeling that their intellectual needs are better satisfied independently, such as through reading. They therefore conclude that social engagement is not a long-term solution for integrating their Fe. INTPs may draw similar conclusions about their romantic partnerships. While they may struggle to live without a romantic partner, they will often conclude that their relationship does not represent the primary solution to integrating their Fe (see *The INTP* for more on this).

INTPs may also try to incorporate the Fe element by working in an organization. Not only does this supply them with basic human interaction, but it can afford them opportunities to engage with likeminded others and achieve recognition for their work. For some INTPs, especially those working in T fields like tech or engineering, this may actually work out pretty well. A potential drawback of this option is when INTPs fail to enjoy or value their work role. In such instances, even the sweetest social trimmings will be incapable of rescuing them from discontentment.

Academia is another alluring option for INTPs. The thought of breathing the air of ideas all day in a community of likeminded others (Fe) is almost a utopian vision for INTPs. It is therefore unfortunate that the modern-day academy is not nearly as idyllic as INTPs might imagine it to be, making it a comfortable and satisfying home for only a small minority of INTPs.

Finally, INTPs may try to integrate their Fe by pursuing it abstractly. Namely, they use Ti and Ne to abstractly explore their F interests. This is undoubtedly why so many INTPs flock to the humanities and social sciences. Abstractly exploring F matters has a number of potential upsides. Because it incorporates Fe, it can supply INTPs with a consistent source of energy and motivation. It also allows them to work independently and creatively, all while still feeling connected to humanity, even if in a rather abstract and indirect way.

To recap, INTPs may try to stimulate or incorporate their Fe in the following ways:

- Finding ways of stoking their feelings (e.g., through music, film, romantic infatuation)
- Seeking affirmation (e.g., being likeable or admirable, pursuing fame or recognition)
- Pursuing N solutions to human problems (e.g., proffering advice or wisdom)

- Engaging with likeminded people (e.g., friends, discussion groups, working in an organization) or partaking in romantic relationships

- Abstractly exploring F interests (e.g., social science, psychology, philosophy, the humanities)

Closing Remarks

Over the last four chapters, we've explored the respective roles of Ti, Ne, Si, and Fe in the INTP quest. Clearly, each of these functions has an important part to play. Ti and Ne probably tell us the most about the overall *structure* of INTPs' purpose. We saw, for instance, how notions such as "independent creative explorer" might capture INTPs' essential typological role.

In our chapter on Si, we looked at the importance of evidence, particularly personal experience, in helping INTPs' clarify and find greater confidence their beliefs and purpose. On the heels of extensive Ne explorations, Si might be seen as playing a *cementing* role. Among other things, it helps recall evidence that is necessary for tracing underlying patterns in INTPs' historical interests or beliefs. It is also useful for reminding INTPs of what has and hasn't worked for them in the past, as illustrated by the maze metaphor.

Finally, in this chapter, we explored Fe and the integral role it plays in supplying motivation and energy for INTPs. While there are a number of ways INTPs may try to incorporate Fe, one of the most common and sustainable ways is through abstractly exploring F topics. Hence, we might suggest that, while Ti and Ne provide the general structure of INTPs' purpose and Si helps to cement or clarify it, Fe may furnish its *inspiration* and potentially contribute to its content.

Notes

1. It is interesting to consider whether INTPs' quest for purpose or meaning is really just an attempt to compensate for their disconnectedness from their own values and emotions. If INTPs somehow managed to better connect with their emotions, would they still feel compelled to avidly search for meaning? Perhaps not. At that point, they would feel more whole and would experience less tension between their Ti and Fe functions.

2. You can find INFP Benjamin David Steele's blog and some of the excerpts I quoted here.

3. It's not that INTPs don't value truth or that INFPs don't value meaning. The point here is that the missing psychological element (e.g., F or T) is often a central concern / interest for each type.

4. For a more in-depth look at the three phases of type development, see *The 16 Personality Types* or *The INTP*. For our purposes in this book, the three phases can be roughly construed as follows: Phase I (childhood), Phase II (differentiation), Phase III (integration).

5. By the second half of life, INTPs may have accumulated sufficient wisdom to qualify as sages, at least with respect to living optimally as INTPs. The problem with their trying to operate as sages in the first half of life is they haven't spent enough time perceiving (Ne-Si) to fully understand human affairs. Without sufficient perception on the front end, their Fe judgments and advice are apt to be less than optimal. Since Ti is their dominant function, less perception is required for INTPs to excel in things like logic or strategizing, which come rather naturally to them. But because their Fe is inferior, it takes much more preparatory work for them to excel, or even achieve competence, in F matters.

PART II

INTPs & Purpose

Expressing and symbolizing human experience through meaningful concepts has long been an aim of religion, philosophy, and psychology. And few concepts seem to do so more powerfully and effectively than that of purpose. The concept of purpose points not only to our experience of purposefulness, but also to our sense of vocation and identity (e.g., "My purpose in life is . . ."). It elegantly marries one of our most poignant inner experiences—that of personal meaning and mission—with our concept of self.

Myriad religious, philosophical, and utopian thinkers have invoked purpose in one guise or another. Many have capitalized on its conceptual breadth and versatility, such as through visions of a divine or universal purpose intersecting with the individual purposes of human beings. These conceptions can be incredibly powerful, prompting individuals to conceive of their lives in terms of numerous layers of purpose—universal, communal, familial, individual, etc. If we associate value with "unity in diversity," as philosopher Robert Nozick suggests, then it is unsurprising that these grand, multi-layered narratives of purpose have captivated human beings for millennia.

As we saw in our introductory chapter, INTPs are bona fide purpose seekers. They want to discover "their thing," a purpose that not only marries their skills and interests, but also serves as an enduring source of inspiration and devotion. Over the next three chapters, we will take a closer look at the nature of INTPs' quest for purpose.

5

IMPORTANCE & ENERGY

In the form of a purpose, INTPs are seeking a certain type of *experience*, one they feel will maximize both their short-term and long-term happiness. Some might describe this as a search for passion, but this doesn't seem entirely appropriate for the thinking-dominant INTP. In my view, the type of experience INTPs are looking for is best described in terms of *importance* and *energy*.

INTPs naturally embrace things that feel important or meaningful to them, and are commensurately repelled by those that don't. It can be a profound struggle for them to perform tasks they view as trivial or meaningless. Recognizing life's brevity, they deplore the thought of wasting time on things that don't matter. This, combined with their penchant for efficiency, contributes to their reputation for being time hoarders. They strive to maximize their alone time in order partake in what they consider to be "important work."

INTPs typically have a decent barometer for what feels (and doesn't feel) important to them. In many cases, such determinations are made outside their conscious awareness. In other words, they may experience something as important without having clear or complete understanding of the criteria being used to make that determination; it feels important, but they can't say exactly why. On other occasions, their evaluative criteria may seem more conscious and a rational explanation (Ti) is available. INTPs who are well-versed in typology may find rational explanations a bit easier to come by, since a sense of importance can often be associated with an inherent need or desire of one of their four functions.[1] Regardless, all INTPs value importance and see it as one of the hallmark features of a suitable purpose.

When INTPs experience something as important, they feel energized and primed for purposeful action. Thus, importance goes hand-in-hand with another core feature of purpose—*energy*. INTPs are generally attuned to their energy levels, including how they are affected by certain ideas, experiences, and individuals. Things believed to augment their energy are welcomed and pursued, while those perceived to diminish their energy are avoided. In short, anticipated energy gains and losses play a prominent role in INTPs' decision-making, including decisions about what might constitute or contribute to their purpose.

Although not an INTP, Frederich Nietzsche is probably the most famous champion of an energy-oriented approach to life, which he described in terms of "the will to power." Another great philosopher, INTP Baruch Spinoza, espoused a similar approach. According to Miguel de Beistegui, "Instead of asking what we ought to do, Spinoza asks what we can do. Ethics is a matter of *power* [i.e., energy], *not duty*."[2] While some personality types approach life and ethics with an eye toward duty, INTPs, in concert with Nietzsche and Spinoza, are apt to "follow the energy." They feel that if they can discover a niche pursuit that consistently satisfies their requirements for energy and importance that they will have, in effect, identified their purpose.

INTPs' concern for energy can be largely associated with their P preference. While their dominant function (Ti) is a judging function, Myers and Briggs classified INTPs as a P type because they extravert their preferred perceiving function (Ne).[3] While this approach has its merits, it can be rather confusing for newcomers to typology. I will thus do my best to contextually clarify when I am emphasizing INTPs' status as dominant judgers (i.e., their Ti dominance) versus highlighting their P *preference*.[4] In the context of this discussion, I am referring to their P preference, which can be associated with spontaneity, impulsivity, and a penchant for instant gratification. It is largely this feature of their personality, seen in all P types, that disposes them to an energy-orientation in their life and purpose. This stands in contrast to the duty-orientation commonly seen in J types.[5]

INTPs' search for an energy-rich purpose can also be tied to their inferior Fe. Even as children, INTPs unwittingly come to associate Fe with energy, discovering that certain Fe ideals and other stoking agents can reliably furnish them with pleasurable emotional highs. Thus, INTPs' energy focus might, to some extent, be seen as an extension of their long-standing habit of seeking Fe-related highs.

Fe also plays a prominent role in INTPs' quest for importance and meaning, which we touched on in the previous chapter. In his thought-provoking book, *Jung's Four and Some Philosophers*, Thomas King argues that the human quest is in large part focused on discovering and integrating the missing / inferior function:

> "The time comes when the individual feels life is empty; something is missing. The original sense of purpose is gone and one is dispirited and confused. At this point the individual feels called to make a difficult search for the rejected (i.e., inferior) function ... The individual sets out on a difficult and unfamiliar journey (e.g., "a sea voyage," "a venture into the forest") to locate the missing function."[6]

It is therefore no surprise that INTPs' quest for purpose is propelled by a concern for characteristically F matters, such as meaning, importance, and significance.

Although INTPs' energy seeking can be associated with impulsivity, instant gratification, and the inferior function, we should avoid hastily labeling it unhealthy or immature. After all, INTPs' pursuit of energy (and purpose generally) constitutes a normal and necessary phase of their type development (Phase II), the goal of which is *differentiation*.

It is the time of life when INTPs are driven to clarify their identity and purpose. And because it constitutes a necessary stage of their development, it cannot be bypassed. Just as we must learn to crawl before walking, INTPs must differentiate their personality (Phase II) before they integrate it (Phase III).[7]

Moreover, as INTPs go about searching for their purpose, they gradually develop a mindset, which we will discuss in Chapter 16, that makes them less dependent on, and less concerned with, impulsive energy.[8] But this must come in its own rightful time. INTPs who are still functioning as seekers (Phase II) typically feel compelled to maintain their energy focus. They seek a purpose that can inspire and motivate them to accomplish great things.

Fortunately, evaluating potential purposes according to their respective levels of energy and importance typically furnishes a satisfying end result for INTPs. As they attend to the types of ideas, interests, and experiences that inspire them, they gradually zero in on a niche pursuit that is worthy of being called their purpose.

Notes

1. While typologists often associate values or value judgments with the feeling function, this is not always helpful. For instance, hunger, an S phenomenon, prompts us to value eating. Similarly, a notion such as fairness might be viewed as a T value insofar as it is rooted in a basic sense of quantity (i.e., equal distribution of something). It therefore seems better to view all the functions as possessing certain needs, desires, and values.

2. de Beistegui, M. *Immanence.* p. 110.

3. See *My True Type* for a more extensive explanation of this issue.

4. When incorporating both Jung and Myers-Briggs, it is important to distinguish the *preferences* (I, E, S, N, T, F, J, P) from the *functions* (Ti, Ne, etc.). Because the Myers-Briggs Type Indicator (MBTI) was modeled on the preferences, this is what most people learn when they are first introduced to type. Those who want to learn more eventually discover the Jungian functions and the functional stack, which furnishes myriad new layers of depth, complexity, and understanding.

5. J types (especially SJs) are well-known for their duty-orientation, that is, for their allegiance to collectively-established rules (Te) or ethics (Fe). By contrast, INTPs (and other P types) are naturally inclined to act according to what is anticipated to maximize their energy in the moment. P types may also act in accordance with their own *self-derived* principles (Ti) or ethics (Fi).

6. King, T. *Jung's Four and Some Philosophers: A Paradigm for Philosophy.*

7. In *The 16 Personality Types*, I describe three phases of type development: childhood (Phase I), differentiation (Phase II), and integration (Phase III). In Phase I, our sense of self is typically rather nebulous and undefined. However, once we start thinking about adulthood and the types of things we might do with our lives, this begins to change. No longer does it feel acceptable to be lumped in with the crowd, that is, to settle for a group-based identity. Instead, we feel compelled to define who we are and what our role is as individuals. The process by which we become, and work to define ourselves as, individuals is called differentiation. Typologically, *differentiation* involves the distinguishing and developing of one's four functions. Because the dominant function is the most conscious and readily accessible function, it is the first to differentiate. The dominant function may also play a prominent role in self-definition. For example, Ti may prompt INTPs to recognize themselves as "thinkers" rather early in life. We will discuss the integration phase of type development in Chapter 16.

8. As INTPs advance toward Phase III of their type development, they may become more dutiful in the sense of subjecting themselves to their own personal principles (Ti) and habits (Si).

6

IDEAS & PURPOSE

Few INTPs would object to the notion that ideas bring a higher level of order, meaning, and significance to human existence. As the German philosopher Schelling observed, "Only ideas provide action with energy and significance."

Ideas are powerful because they represent idealized alternatives (N) to what currently exists (S). By juxtaposing N ideals with S reality, we create gradients that are dense with potential energy. Focusing on an imagined goal or ideal can go a long way in energizing and inspiring us. Don't like your life as it is? Start by imagining something better.

Ideas also have a close relationship to movement (read up on the "ideomotor effect" for more on this) and are therefore integral to life processes. This even holds for subconscious ideas, which is why ideas can be seen as playing a central role in the operations and evolution of even the most rudimentary life forms.[1] In short, ideas are fundamental to life, growth, and vitality.

Recognizing the close relationship between ideas and vital processes helps us understand why depression is viewed as a non-optimal state of being. If the ideas associated with depression serve to diminish movement and life energy, it is not difficult to see why depression might be perceived as a threat to survival.[2]

Jung was no stranger to the power and importance of ideas. In discussing the "primordial image," by which he meant something very similar to an idea, he wrote:

> "[It] gives a coordinating and coherent meaning both to sensuous and inner perceptions . . . and in this way frees psychic energy from its bondage to sheer uncomprehended perception. At the same time, it links the energies released by the perception of stimuli to a definite meaning, which then guides action along paths corresponding to this meaning."[3]

Jung makes two noteworthy observations in this quote. The first is the close relationship between ideas and energy. He suggests that ideas help free up psychic energy, which accords with my assertion that ideas can augment our energy levels. Second, Jung points out that ideas can funnel that energy in a specific direction. In other words, they can serve as goals and guideposts for purposeful action. Thus, ideas play a significant role in energy and self-direction, both of which INTPs see as fundamental elements of purpose.

Characteristics of Powerful Ideas

With respect to purpose, the degree to which we consider a given idea to be valuable hinges on its perceived importance and its effects on our energy levels. Generally speaking, the ideas that furnish the most energy might be considered the most valuable. But what factors determine the impact of an idea on our energy levels?

From a type perspective, we might hypothesize that the most powerful ideas are those that resonate with all four of our functions. On this view, religious and political frameworks are powerful because they are broad and versatile enough to satisfy the S, N, T, and F functions (and types). Not only do these frameworks cater to the individual needs of each function, but they also manage to unify them. In so doing, they represent potential solutions to the problem of psychological integration, which of course is deeply attractive to the human psyche. It is therefore not surprising that religion and politics are viewed as important (and sensitive) topics.

Especially early in life, INTPs can be drawn to certain religious or political ideologies. But because they are disposed to constantly questioning and revising their beliefs, they often struggle to consistently commit to any collective ideology—political, religious, or otherwise. In time, most move away from popular ideologies in favor of an admixture of ideas that personally resonates with them. They seek ideas that are reasonable (Ti), novel and versatile (Ne), relevant to their experience (Si), as well as meaningful and inspiring (Fe). Moreover, INTPs prefer working with ideas packaged in the form of *concepts*.

INTPs' Penchant for Concepts

INTPs are commonly characterized as *philosophers*, while TJ types are commonly portrayed as *scientists*. Underlying these characterizations is the recognition that INTPs and TJs prefer rather different approaches to working with ideas and understanding reality.

As devotees to the extraverted variety of thinking (Te), TJs function more like scientists, opting for precise terms and definitions with *only one meaning*. While INTPs share TJs concern for clarity of expression, they often feel bored or stifled by the terminological restrictions imposed by Te. Their Ne demands more imaginative space and freedom than Te is willing to concede.

To further elucidate this matter, we will now turn to the work of French philosopher and INTP, Gilles Deleuze. In *What is Philosophy?*, Deleuze and his sidekick, Felix Guattari, contrast the aims and approaches of philosophy versus science. They suggest that scientists deal with *functions* (not to be confused with Jung's functions), which fix the relationship among variables rather than allowing for freedom and variation. Philosophers, by contrast, prefer working with *concepts*. One of Deleuze's most celebrated ideas is the notion that the purpose of philosophy (or perhaps more accurately, INTP philosophy) is to create concepts. Instead of fixing the variables and definitions, philosophers accept, and even appreciate, a certain measure of vagueness or versatility, including allowing their concepts to have *multiple connotations* (another INTP philosopher, Georges Canguilhem, referred to this as "theoretical polyvalence"). Deleuze and Guattari also suggest that philosophers are less concerned with hierarchical structuring. Although they enjoy making connections among concepts, many do so in a less systematic or rigorous way than scientists. This jives with my observation in *My True Type* that Ne is more weblike in its workings, while Te is more hierarchical.

Philosophers and scientists also differ in the underlying motivations for their work. According to Deleuze and Guattari:

> "Philosophy does not consist of knowing, and is not inspired
> by truth. Rather, it is categories like 'interesting, remarkable,
> and important' that determine its success or failure."[4]

Here, I see the authors defending the divergent nature of Ne and its association with creative inspiration, as well as Fe's concern for meaning and significance. If we contrast this with the needs of TJs' Te, we are confronted with distinct motivational differences between these types. Namely, INTPs / philosophers strive to explore and express ideas in creative and versatile ways (Ne), whereas TJs / scientists work to strictly define and hierarchically situate all variables in a more rigid fashion (Te).

What Deleuze seemed to understand, perhaps as clearly as anyone, is that philosophers (and INTPs) experience great pleasure and satisfaction from exploring, connecting, and creating concepts. I think it is safe to say that no other personality type enjoys working with concepts more than the INTP.

But why concepts? What is it about concepts that captivates INTPs? The short answer is that concepts are more conducive than say, tightly structured systems, to the workings of Ti and Ne. They are vague and fluid enough to allow Ne to make plenty of creative connections and associations, yet structured enough to satisfy Ti's need for ideational order and concision.

The importance of concepts to INTPs is nicely illustrated in Robert Pirsig's classic philosophical novel, *Zen and the Art of Motorcycle Maintenance*. In an accessible and interesting way, Pirsig (definitely an ITP, likely an INTP) retraces his own philosophical journey. Over the course of the book, he explores his thoughts and experiences with numerous philosophical concepts and schools of thought. The book culminates with Pirsig's discovery of what for him represented the ultimate concept—*quality*. This revelation was in many regards the capstone experience of his life. In the concept of quality, he found a place where truth and meaning, art and science, beauty and technology, T and F, could be integrated. Pirsig's book aptly exemplifies the INTP quest, including their search for purpose by way of concepts. We will further discuss Pirsig's book and his concept of quality in Chapter 8.

Self-Concept

One of the most important concepts for INTPs is their self-concept. They sense that understanding themselves—their interests, values, and abilities—is an important prerequisite to finding their life's purpose. Toward this end, they may subject themselves to countless self-tests and inventories—personality, interests, values, IQ, etc.—in hopes of clarifying their identity and personal strengths. With each new assessment comes a sense of hope and anticipation of learning something new and interesting about themselves.

To further clarify their self-concept, INTPs may study the lives of others, whether in real life or through film, fiction, biographies, etc. In doing so, they may ask themselves questions such as: How much do I like, value, or identify with this individual? How are we similar (or different)? What can I learn from him or her? Does this person inspire me? Is he or she worth emulating?

Through these explorations, INTPs not only seek to understand their *actual self*, but also strive to clarify who they'd like to be become—their *ideal self*. They want to hammer down who they are and what they're good at, while also envisioning and advancing toward a more ideal version of themselves. Again, this is why ideas are such an integral part of their purpose, supplying the vision, impetus, and direction for their lives.

Archetypes

Archetypes are conceptions of the foundational character roles of humanity. If we were to analyze a group of people or characters and look for common roles and patterns, we could identify a variety of archetypes. Some of the more commonly proposed archetypes are creator, destroyer, mother, warrior, seeker / explorer, trickster, hero, sage, ruler, and magician.

While there is certainly significant overlap between archetypes and personality types, archetypes do a better job of capturing and conveying the central role of an individual. Knowing, for instance, that an individual has adopted the mother archetype, may tell us more (at least at first glance) about her primary life role than knowing her personality type.

For similar reasons, many people have found the Enneagram to be a powerful typological framework. The Enneagram types are centered on a single motivation or life role and in this sense resemble archetypes. The Enneagram types, as described by Riso and Hudson (my preferred Enneagram authors), include the Reformer (1), Helper (2), Achiever (3), Individualist (4), Investigator (5), Loyalist (6), Enthusiast (7), Leader (8), and Peacemaker (9). As you can see, these map rather well onto certain archetypes such as the ruler (8), mother (2), seeker / explorer (7), creator (4), etc. Because archetypes and Enneagram types utilize the sorts of concepts INTPs are drawn to (e.g., those with versatile meanings and connotations), INTPs may find them useful and inspiring.

It may also be helpful, for our purposes, to draw a line of contrast between archetypes, which represent broad "life roles" (Fe), and conventional careers, which involve specific "work roles" (Te). Types using the Te-Fi function pair (i.e., TJs and FPs), typically have an easier time functioning in conventional careers, because their use of Te makes them sympathetic to standardized protocols and procedures. Types employing the Ti-Fe function pair (i.e., TPs and FJs), by contrast, feel less at home with standardized procedures, preferring instead to informally negotiate solutions ("a wink and a handshake" (Fe)) or manufacture their own way of doing things (Ti). At some point, this may prompt them to stop seeking their purpose in the form of a pre-existing career path and to instead focus on finding the right archetype or self-concept. They sense that doing so might furnish them with the direction and inspiration they need to craft a purposeful life, however unconventional.

INTP Archetypes

If there is one thing INTPs know about themselves, it is their penchant for introverted thinking. When this is combined with Fe, they may be compelled to adopt the sage archetype, seeing themselves as seekers and dispensers of life wisdom. But, as we discussed in Chapter 4, this may not be their best-fit role, especially early in life. It therefore seems advisable for INTPs to consider other archetypes, such as that of creator, explorer, philosopher, or investigator.

When first encountering the creator archetype, our first inclination might be to think of artists. To some extent, this is justified, since artists are in many ways the purest embodiment of unfettered creativity. But what about architects, inventors, engineers, entrepreneurs, software developers, non-fiction writers, and the like? These are the T correlates to F artists, all of which may be animated by the creator archetype.

With respect to the explorer archetype, we saw in Chapter 2 how INTPs are driven by a need for exploration. They particularly enjoy exploring, analyzing, and connecting ideas. While explorers can be found in both the sciences and humanities, INTPs are more often drawn to the humanities or social sciences because of the pull of their inferior Fe.

Most archetype resources do not include the philosopher archetype. This has always seemed a bit curious to me, considering that it may be the archetype that best captures the essential role of the INTP. This oversight may have stemmed from the conflation of the philosopher and sage roles in ancient societies. Or, perhaps the philosopher role seems too modern and therefore unworthy of archetype status. Regardless, if we consider that the majority of famous philosophers were INTPs and that most INTPs enjoy philosophy (or at least think like philosophers), we would be remiss not to include the philosopher as one of our top INTP archetypes.

In light of the importance of the philosopher archetype for INTPs, we can further appreciate the work that Deleuze and Guattari have done in teasing out the differences between philosophers and scientists. Deleuze also likened philosophers to artists, probably because both philosophers and artists commonly use Ne. Along these lines, I have come to see the INTP philosopher as doing something very similar to what the INFP novelist does.[5] Both explore and analyze the human condition, with the primary difference being that novelists conduct their experiments and explorations with characters, whereas philosophers do so with concepts. Both characters and concepts can serve as consolidated centers of meaning and insight into the human condition. We might therefore view the philosopher as a sort of "concept novelist," or more generally, a "concept artist."

Finally, INTPs may resonate with the investigator archetype, especially as outlined by Riso and Hudson in their book, *Personality Types*. The notion of investigator is similar to that of explorer, but has a stronger T connotation. It also resembles the philosopher archetype, but carries the advantage of being less specific with respect to its subject matter. It therefore deserves a place among INTPs' top potential archetypes.

Closing Thoughts

In exploring an array of ideas, concepts, and archetypes, INTPs seek ways of better defining or representing, in their own minds, who they are and what their purpose is. They seek to discern *holistic essences* (Chapter 1), which means working with ideas that are at once foundational and holistic. Archetypes are a good example of this. Not only do they convey the essence of an individual's life role, but they are holistic and versatile enough to avoid being too restrictive or unidimensional. In Chapter 8, we will explore additional concepts that INTPs may find helpful in clarifying their purpose.

Notes

1. My view is that all the functions—T, F, S, and N—have rudimentary precursors in lower life forms. Hence, even bacteria can be said as having ideas (N), even if rather different from human ideas. The ideomotor phenomenon suggests that ideas precede and precipitate movement. The mental image / idea of a movement serves as its guide and impetus. Moreover, these ideas need not be conscious to exert their effects. We should therefore be careful not to rule out the role of ideas in lower life forms simply because their ideas are not conscious. The inner world (IN) of lower life forms is just as real and important as their outer / observable elements (ES). We will further explore this topic in Chapter 10.

2. But why do we value life over death? Why do most human beings want to live as long as possible? The answer may be as simple as this: If human beings did not value life, there is a good chance we would have already gone extinct. We might also speculate that one of the general characteristics of life is a desire

to live. Perhaps this fundamental desire contributed to the emergence of life from non-life, as well as its evolution.

3. Jung, C.G. *Psychological Types*. Para 749.

4. Deleuze, G and Guattari, F. *What is Philosophy?* 1994.

5. It is instructive to observe the significant typological similarities between INTPs and INFPs. Both use introverted judging (Ti or Fi), followed by Ne and Si. In my view, this similarity in typological structure suggests a similarity in the general role / purpose of these two types.

7

THE I-E STRUGGLE

In the last couple chapters, we explored INTPs' quest for importance, energy, and guiding concepts, all of which can be roughly construed as introverted concerns. But even the most introverted INTPs feel compelled, at some point, to consider how their purpose might impact, or otherwise connect up with, the outside world.

As we've seen, INTPs have a strong need to follow their own inner (i.e., introverted) compass wherever it leads. But like other introverts, they cannot merely dismiss the needs and desires of their extraverted functions. Most INTPs learn through experience that completely ignoring the outside world is not a viable option for them. No matter how hard they try to function as "islands," they are always brought back to the fact that they need to relate to someone or something outside themselves. At minimum, they want others to acknowledge and appreciate the fruits of their introverted labor. INTPs must also find ways of earning an income, which clearly requires some level of engagement with the outside world.

The introduction of extraverted (E) concerns into INTPs' search for purpose almost always makes the process more difficult and complicated. Among other things, it causes INTPs to feel inwardly divided, unsure of the degree to which they should compromise their introverted self for the sake of extraverted rewards. But the outside world can also be a powerful motivator for INTPs, especially early in life, due to its association with their Fe ideals.

INTPs who grant too much attention to E matters, such as over-emphasizing profits or how others are responding to their work, may be nagged by the sense that they are acting inauthentically or fraudulently. They may feel that their work fails to reflect their true self (i.e., their introverted self), or that they have somehow lost or unduly compromised themselves for the sake of external gain. INTPs who attempt to ignore E matters may also run into problems. They may suffer from apathy, depression, or nihilism, perhaps feeling that if no one is there to appreciate their work, then "What's the point of doing it at all?"

Most INTPs are familiar with both of these extremes. They are particularly well-acquainted with the side-effects of extreme introversion, since isolation and self-preservation is their default coping mechanism. But they also know how dirty it feels to "sell out," that is, to forsake their own beliefs or principles for the sake of pleasing or placating others.

This I-E struggle often rears its head when INTPs are trying to clarify their niche purpose and target audience / market. On the one hand, they may worry that if they allow their interests to become too obscure or esoteric (I) that they will fail to capture a sufficiently large (E) audience or make enough money. On the other hand, if they stray too far from their core interests in pursuit of popular appeal, the burden of inauthenticity and disingenuousness may grow unbearable. At either extreme, their energy levels may drop to undesirable levels.[1]

Many people have observed that, once artists become famous, the quality of their work starts to suffer. The typological explanation for this is that their usual introverted focus has become disrupted or subsumed by extraverted concerns, impairing their ability to find their typical artistic groove. These sorts of concerns may inspire INTPs to establish a clear line of division between their purpose-related pursuits (I) and their source of income (E). Generally, this means working a "day job" for income and pursuing their purpose on the side. This allows their purpose to remain pure and untainted by E concerns.

In my experience, the benefits of this sort of arrangement can be substantial enough to make a day job tolerable, perhaps even enjoyable, for INTPs. I have personally made it a practice to write for several hours in the morning, when my mind is fresh, rejuvenated, and less burdened with outside concerns. I then head off to my job, often feeling positive and energized after sustained employment of my Ti and Ne. With that said, the anxieties, frustrations, or perceived meaninglessness of certain jobs may at times prove unbearable for INTPs. In such instances, INTPs' desire to find ways of monetizing their niche interest may grow stronger and, with it, the sense of I-E conflict outlined above.

Changing the World

Another common E interest among INTPs is wanting to "change the world." This sort of idealism is particularly prevalent among INTPs in early adulthood, before the realities of life have become fully apparent.

The "change the world" notion can be associated with extraverted judging and, therefore, with INTPs' inferior Fe. Changing oneself, by contrast, would correspond to introverted judging (Ti), making it a far more reasonable goal for INTPs. As Aldous Huxley once remarked, "There is only one corner of the universe you can be certain of improving, and that's your own self." While INTPs may at times envy the sense of mission evinced by famous reformers, they often end up feeling inauthentic and unfulfilled in such roles.

In order for the change-agent role to be consistently rewarding for INTPs, it must entail plenty of opportunities for new investigations, problem-solving, or creative thinking. In other words, it must sufficiently stimulate their Ti and Ne. Moreover, as a general rule, it is best for INTPs to focus less on E outcomes (e.g., directly changing the world) and more on the intrinsic value derived from exploration, investigation, and creative expression. While it is true that INTPs such as Kant and Einstein changed the world, this was not, from what I can discern, their primary intention. Like most INTPs, they didn't know if, or exactly how, their work would effect change. So rather than focusing directly on procuring external change (Fe), INTPs are wise to follow their introverted interests, allowing the extraverted chips to fall where they may.

Notes

1. To learn more about the challenges involved with reconciling the I and E elements, see my Personality Junkie blog posts: The Introvert's Dilemma and Introverts' vs. Extraverts' Career Paths.

PART III

INTPs & Philosophy

You may recall that this book strives to clarify INTPs' understanding of three core matters: their self / personality, their purpose, and their philosophy. Since it is now time to turn our sights toward the latter, it is helpful to recall our reasons for doing so. Namely, for INTPs to discern their purpose, they must not only come to an understanding of themselves, but also of the world or universe as a whole. This, among other things, compels them to take up investigations of a religious or philosophical nature.

To kick off our foray into all things philosophical, Chapter 8 explores some concepts and approaches INTPs might find useful in establishing their philosophical foundations. Chapters 9-13 enumerate some of INTPs' core philosophical propensities, as well as philosophical paths they may find interesting or meaningful.

8

FOUNDATIONS

As expressed in our introductory chapter, in order to formulate their purpose, INTPs must first come to an understanding of their core self and core philosophy. In using the term "core philosophy," I am not necessarily referring to a thorough philosophical understanding or grand philosophical system, although some INTPs may aspire toward these things. Rather, I suggest that a core philosophy should entail *whatever the self deems most relevant and important to its purposes.*

Johann Gottlieb Fichte (INTP) was one of the first philosophers to take an explicitly self-oriented philosophical approach. Henry Aiken nicely summarizes Fichte's perspective in his book, *The Age of Ideology*:

> "From Fichte's standpoint, it is pointless to ask in the manner of a scientist, whether there is an external world beyond experience, or whether there is a God. Such a way of putting these questions entirely misrepresents their significance, which is practical, not theoretical . . . It is the Self and its demands which provide the only possible warrant for believing in God . . . Imagine an ordinary fellow who is at first stimulated by, then increasingly perplexed by, controversies over the question whether there is an external world. At last

he bursts out with the apparently unphilosophical question, "What does it matter whether there is an external world or not?" . . . The question for Fichte, is not so much whether something is "there," but whether there is any practical point in saying so . . ."[1]

The existentialist philosopher Soren Kierkegaard saw things essentially the same way. Kierkegaard maintained that the sole purpose of philosophizing was to discover ways of better navigating one's existential situation and to cultivate a more meaningful life. In his view, the value of an idea or philosophy rested entirely on its perceived value or utility to the individual. In concert with Fichte, he envisaged philosophy as an essentially practical and self-enriching enterprise.

By identifying their ultimate philosophical aim as practical / personal in nature, INTPs can more easily shed unrealistic or unnecessary expectations regarding the size and scope of their philosophical efforts. Namely, it can be easy for INTPs to believe that, because their type is associated with thinking and philosophizing, they are somehow obligated to function as a systematic philosopher in the way of Kant or Aristotle, or as a grand synthesizer in the way of Hegel. Not only can these grandiose expectations lead INTPs to feel overwhelmed, but also to forget why they started philosophizing in the first place, which was to satisfy their own personal interests and curiosities.

To be clear, I am not suggesting that INTPs should (or even can) completely ignore extant ideas or objective knowledge, or retreat to magical or premodern thinking. Even if they tried, they could never convince themselves that the earth is flat or that Santa Claus is real. Their immersion in modern culture, combined with their natural propensity for critical thinking (Ti) and need to explore a broad range of ideas (Ne), is typically sufficient to keep them from losing contact with external realities.

Philosophy: More than Truth-Seeking?

In Chapter 6, we first encountered Deleuze and Guattari's assertion that "Philosophy does not consist of knowing, and is not inspired by truth. Rather, it is categories like 'interesting, remarkable, and important' that determine its success or failure." In making this claim, I believe the authors were attempting to convey something similar to what I have been working to articulate, which is that INTPs philosophize in order to meet the needs of the self, including needs that extend beyond truth and into the realm of the "interesting, remarkable, and important."

With that said, we must also recognize that when INTPs' are wielding Ti, they have a strong sense that their logic is valid and is therefore operating in the direction of truth. Hence, I am inclined to disagree with Deleuze and Guattari's assertion that philosophers (or INTPs) are not inspired by truth. It seems more accurate to say that a philosopher's work is inspired by truth insofar as he *needs* or *values* truth.[2] To this I might add that the degree to which an INTP uses Ti in an unbiased way (assuming that is a real possibility) will reflect his level of concern for truth.

In my view, INTPs philosophize in order to satisfy whatever need they have to explore what is true (Ti), interesting / mysterious (Ne), historically relevant (Si), or important / meaningful (Fe). I think this is the reality that Deleuze and Guattari intuitively grasped and were attempting to explicate. They realized that restricting the philosopher's concern to truth failed to capture what is in fact a broader or more holistic set of aims.

On the whole, I think Deleuze and Guattari have done INTPs a great favor. Their work, in combination with that of Fichte, Kierkegaard, and others, can have a liberating effect on INTPs' philosophical outlook and work, allowing them to excise any undue limitations or expectations they've placed on themselves. This clears more imaginative space for Ne to roam, explore, and create.

Of course, whenever INTPs introduce more variables (e.g., the needs of more functions) into the equation, it becomes more difficult for them to find unifying themes or essences. So while they can appreciate more philosophical freedom, it may fail to furnish them with a clearer sense of identity and purpose. Nevertheless, I do not consider this problem insurmountable.

As we've seen, INTPs feel compelled to clarify their purpose *conceptually*. This includes working to identify core concepts that embody their ultimate concerns. At minimum, INTPs seek concepts that incorporate their concern for truth (Ti) and meaning (Fe), but also leave plenty of room for freedom and mystery (Ne). Among the top contenders in this respect is Robert Pirsig's concept of *quality* as explored in his classic book, *Zen and the Art of Motorcycle Maintenance*.

Pirsig's Concept of Quality

According to Pirsig, what a good mechanic (T), a good philosopher (N), and a good poet (F) have in common is the quality of their work. He asserts that we tend to know quality when we see it and even considers it a universal human value. While the latter point is certainly debatable, this is not our primary concern here. Rather, our concern is the degree to which the concept of quality satisfactorily embodies and reconciles the needs of INTPs' Ti, Ne, and Fe.

Pirsig makes a strong case for quality being an inherent concern and attribute of Ti. He artfully paints the process of motorcycle maintenance, which can be construed as a Ti activity because of its demand for situational / holistic logic, as a predominantly qualitative enterprise. While it is true that a mechanic must employ some measure of left-brained logic, such as his knowledge of the hierarchical structure and workings of the motorcycle, he works largely by "feel." In other words, an expert mechanic knows a well-tuned bike when he sees, hears, and experiences it. The fact that a bike satisfies certain diagnostic tests (Te) does not mean it is well-tuned. Rather, expert tuning requires a holistic or qualitative approach, that is, interaction with the subjectivity of the mechanic, in order to facilitate the optimal balance and coordination of all the parts and systems.

But what about when Ti (in conjunction with Ne) is handling abstract ideas (e.g., philosophizing)? Would it still be well-described by the concept of quality in this case? I would say so and suspect Pirsig would agree. INTPs' natural mode of thinking is more holistic than it is linear or quantitative (Te). They are not naturally systematic in their approach, but apply their reasoning as it seems appropriate to a particular problem or context. Their thinking tends to be more impromptu and situational (or what Lenore Thomson calls "field dependent") than comprehensive, as illustrated by their penchant for devising clever hacks and workarounds.

With further analysis, we can identify additional points of overlap between the mechanic (ISTP) and the more abstract thinker (INTP).[3] What is the mechanic's goal? Clearly one of them is a finely-tuned motorcycle. But if we look a little closer, we find that the mechanic is also seeking pleasure in his work; not only is he tuning motorcycles, but enhancing the quality of his life in the process. Likewise, the abstract thinker lives, and discovers how to live better, through philosophizing. Therefore, the common link between the mechanic and the abstract thinker is a concern for quality—in both life and work. These and other observations convinced Pirsig of the power and wisdom that the concept of quality could supply, ultimately compelling him to embrace it as his central concept.

While not stated explicitly in his book, I suspect that Pirsig realized, at least at some level, that one of quality's greatest advantages was its conceptual versatility. Because it can refer to anything that is good, valuable, or excellent, it can easily accommodate T, F, S, and N things. Even experiences such as unity and mystery can find a ready home under the quality umbrella. And if this weren't already enough, quality can also connote the qualitative (i.e., inner / subjective) realm of human experience, which INTPs love to explore and contemplate. Thus, quality more than satisfies INTPs' criteria for conceptual versatility, making it an attractive option for those seeking a foundational concept for their lives.

Another contender for INTPs' core concept is wisdom. Wisdom elegantly marries their concern for truth (Ti), mystery (Ne), and meaning (Fe). It can also help distinguish INTPs' overarching purpose from that of TJ types. Namely, INTPs might be characterized as seekers of wisdom (e.g., philosophers) and TJs as seekers of knowledge (e.g., scientists).

It probably goes without saying that purpose is another powerful concept for INTPs, beautifully integrating T utility, N ideals, and F meaning and significance. It also sports a stronger sense of directionality than either quality or wisdom.

INTPs may also take interest in INTP theologian Paul Tillich's notion of "ultimate concern." As we've seen, INTPs look for broad and versatile concepts, and Tillich does not disappoint in this respect. A "concern" can be either subjective (e.g., "I am deeply concerned.") or objective (e.g., "Our primary concern in today's discussion is . . ."). Philosophically, it can be used in an existential sense (e.g., the ultimate concern of the individual) or a metaphysical / theological sense (e.g., God as an ultimate concern). In reading some of Tillich's commentary on this matter, he had clearly invested ample time searching for such a potent and capable concept. While I must admit that I failed to notice its versatility when I first encountered it, I now see it as a rather brilliant way of bridging INTPs' existential and metaphysical interests.

Just to be clear, embracing a central concept should not be seen as negating the need for, or value of, other concepts. After all, exploring an array of concepts (Ne) is a common source of enjoyment and purpose for INTPs. So instead of seeing their primary concept as replacing other concepts, INTPs might view it as a sort of conceptual center around which other concepts will find their orbit.

Wisdom

INTPs who adopt quality as their core concept might conceive their purpose as "moving things in the direction of quality." This is a very broad and holistic notion, emphasizing the overarching effects of one's actions. But because quality incorporates a diversity of factors (as all broad concepts do), there are times when some factors must be deemphasized or compromised to maximize the overall quality of an outcome. For instance, some situations may demand that meaning or significance (F) take precedence over truth or accuracy (T) in order for quality to be maximized. In other cases, the reverse will be true.

But how is it, exactly, that we know what to prioritize to ensure quality is maximized? Where does this wisdom come from? Among other things, wisdom entails knowing which function(s) to use in order to maximize quality in a given situation. Our sense of discernment is informed by our past experiences (Si), including what we've learned from our mistakes. It is also influenced by our typological preferences (e.g., T types are apt to use T in more situations than F types might). But wisdom seems to involve something more than a referencing of our type preferences and personal experiences. Jung felt it necessary to posit the existence of another factor—the "transcendent function"—whose chief role was to wisely select and coordinate the functions.

People typically respond to the notion of transcendent wisdom in one of two ways. Those bent toward scientific materialism tend to deny its existence, perhaps arguing that all human choices can or will ultimately be explained neurologically. In their view, positing the existence of a transcendent factor is unscientific and in all likelihood unnecessary. The second response, typically proffered by those with a religious or spiritual inclination, is that wisdom can ultimately be traced back to some sort of immaterial mind, spirit, or divinity. In my experience, many INTPs, included a number of INTP philosophers (e.g., Spinoza, Fichte, Hegel, Bergson, etc.) lean toward this latter view.

Since its sources or mechanisms often escape the spotlight of our consciousness, we often consider wisdom a "mysterious" phenomenon. And whenever we deem something mysterious or impenetrable, the idea of a divine force or being is often not far away. Throughout this book, I have suggested that one's purpose will (and should) reflect the needs and demands of the self, including one's personality type. But if we grant the potential reality of an immaterial spirit, mind, or divinity, we are forced to consider whether our purpose is ultimately personal, or whether it might be better conceived in spiritual terms. To put it another way, should we be turning to psychology to understand our purpose, or are we better off focusing our efforts on religion and metaphysics? Most INTPs ask themselves this very question, in some form or another, as they attempt to discern the appropriate starting point for their philosophy.

A religious individual might argue that the key to wise living is understanding and submitting to God's will. Consideration of individual differences, such as one's personality type, is therefore of secondary concern. To throw a wrench into this argument, we might consider whether it would be wise for an INTP to work full-time in a childcare center. Even if this unfortunate INTP happened to be zen enough to handle such a daunting task, it certainly wouldn't capitalize on his natural abilities or interests. This illustrates the contribution of typology to wisdom. Even if God were a reality in the universe, this would not obviate the necessity of factoring individual differences into our wisdom equation.

We could likewise criticize typologists who overemphasize the dominant function or underemphasize the importance of discernment and properly balancing the functions. In other words, by keying in on the signature strengths of an individual's personality, they may overlook the discerning and integrative element of wisdom.

Closing Remarks

We began this chapter by suggesting that INTPs might be wise to view their philosophical efforts as directed toward satisfying their own subjective needs. Doing so has many ostensible advantages. With respect to the history of philosophy, INTPs will find plenty of moral support and role models among the existentialists, as well as to some extent, the pragmatists. Both existentialists and pragmatists can be seen as sidestepping Kant's *Critique of Pure Reason* (which cast doubt on the prospect of ascertaining unmediated, objective knowledge[4]) by emphasizing philosophy's value as a practical or personal (rather than ontological) tool. This can be an effective way for INTPs to clear the philosophical space required to build a *positive* or *constructive* philosophy, even in an age characterized by relativism, skepticism, pluralism, and deconstructionism. It permits them to move beyond doubt and skepticism in order to embrace a philosophy that is personally useful and meaningful.

Notes

1. Aiken, H. *The Age of Ideology*. pp. 54-55.

2. For the most part, this book uses plural pronouns for the sake of gender neutrality. However, in cases where singular pronouns are called for, I have opted to employ the pronoun "he" for the sake of consistency and parsimony. I hope my female readers will accept this decision and recognize its pragmatic basis.

3. Both INTPs and ISTPs use Ti as their dominant function. Hence, the comparison between the hands-on ITP (i.e., the ISTP mechanic) and the more abstract ITP (i.e., the INTP philosopher).

4. Kant's most famous and influential work, *Critique of Pure Reason*, cast doubt on the human mind's ability to accurately ascertain the true nature of things. Kant argued that we can't see things but through the subjective filters of the mind. In his view, obtaining unadulterated objective knowledge is an impossibility for human knowers. Prior to Kant, thinkers had merely accused each other of seeing things the wrong way and then proceeded to explain why their own viewpoints were superior. Most believed they could enjoy full

access to "the mind of God," one only needed to discover the optimal way of doing so. In short, subjectivity was recognized as problematic, but not insurmountable. With Kant, the problem of subjectivity was made absolute and the seeds for a new age were sewn, one characterized by epistemic uncertainty and relativism. This represented a sea-change for human beings, who had long assumed they possessed (or could obtain) certain and absolute knowledge. Fortunately, Fichte (who was actually a student of Kant) and others realized that Kant's critique presented no real barrier to the establishment of a meaningful personal philosophy.

9

PHILOSOPHY & RELIGION

INTPs are metaphysically, if not spiritually, inclined. While some will headquarter their spiritual interests in traditional religion and theology, the arrow of INTPs' developmental progression points away from traditional religion (at least in its most conservative forms) and toward a broader spiritual, philosophical, and / or psychological understanding. This progression is unpacked and substantiated in James Fowler's "Stages of Faith," which depict the developmental transition away from traditional religion and toward more universal and demythologized perspectives. While Fowler's stages are by no means limited to INTPs, the nature of INTPs' personality makes them more likely than most other types to progress in their spiritual or philosophical understanding.

Religion, Philosophy, & INTPs

Philosophy and religion / theology are similar insofar as they are concerned with the metaphysical aspects of reality, as well as with the existential predicament of human beings. They tend to part ways, however, when it comes their epistemologies and worldviews.

Religion, at least in its Western monotheistic conception, emphasizes tradition, authority, and "special" (i.e., supernatural) revelation as conduits for truth. Divine secrets are believed to have been revealed to a handful of saints or prophets, and religious subscribers are expected to have "faith" that such revelations are true and trustworthy.

Philosophers, by contrast, are typically far less sympathetic to claims of supernatural revelation. For them, the idea that truth is not revealed or accessible at all times and to all people, but only to specially chosen prophets, contravenes their desire for fairness as well as for consistency in the natural world. In concert with scientists, they believe that truth should be discernable from the evidence before or within us—no angels or miracles required. Allowing for arbitrary, supernatural interventions goes against their desire for consistency and a certain measure of predictability in nature. This attitude is well embodied in Einstein's famous quip that "God doesn't play dice." Einstein expected the cosmos to behave in reliable and predictable ways, especially when his Ti was at the helm.[1]

It can also be hard for philosophers not to see organized religion as a safe haven for people who are afraid or unable to think for themselves. After all, using faith as one's primary epistemology is akin to saying: "Since I'm not confident that I can discover truth on my own, I'm going to trust someone else to do it for me." If one wished to conserve cognitive resources, exercising faith would seem to be a good option. But because philosophers derive great satisfaction from independently exploring truth, few are willing to let faith lead the way. If they do, it's usually only temporary, before reason once again takes the reins.

Despite the centrality of faith to religion, it is typically buttressed by other epistemologies or justifications. After all, if faith was one's only tool, there would be no real justification for being a Christian versus a Muslim. Without other forms of evidence or argument, believers would be forced to concede that their reasons for choosing their religion were entirely arbitrary or circumstantial. Again, this sort of randomness tends to be off-putting to philosophers, who insist on having good reasons and justifications for their beliefs. Faith is the least preferred epistemology for philosophers, at least consciously.[2] They prefer to rely on reason, intuition, and experience for discerning truth. If an idea fails to pass the test of reason, it is typically jettisoned immediately.

INTPs are naturally inclined to operate more like philosophers than traditional religious subscribers. While most INTPs are animated by what we might call a religious spirit or impulse (i.e., a concern for a more meaningful, purposeful, or spiritual life), their Ti is reluctant to place its trust in tradition, authority, or blind faith. As the most independent and anti-authoritarian of all the functions, Ti insists on developing and referencing its own reasons and justifications. In the spirit of the philosopher, INTPs venture to build their beliefs from the ground up, enlisting the aid of reason (Ti), intuition (Ne), and, to some extent, evidence and experience (Si).[3]

Examining Theism

If we are to operate effectively as philosophers, we must begin by considering some foundational issues and questions. Among these is this notion of theism, which most INTPs, especially those raised in Western cultures, feel compelled to evaluate rather early in their intellectual journey. Coming to terms with theism is an important step for INTPs, as it will profoundly affect the way they see the world and humanity, as well as their own purpose in the world. In this discussion, my use of the term theism is intended to broadly connote the monotheistic conception (e.g., an omnibenevolent, omnipotent, and omniscient God) traditionally espoused by religions such as Christianity, Judaism, and Islam.

In considering the potential merits of theism, INTPs might start by asking themselves why God, if he (or she / it) existed, might choose to create other sentient beings. One of the more common Christian responses to this question is "for his own glory." In other words, God created other beings in the hope that they would bow down and worship him. To the INTP mind, this response is profoundly dubious, effectively painting God as a divine narcissist or egoist. This conception also casts significant doubt on God's omnibenevolence, which is one of the three signature features of the monotheistic God. Moreover, it suggests that God is lacking something vital (e.g., self-worth, self-esteem) that can only be supplied from without. This contradicts another theistic assumption, which is that God is characteristically whole and complete on his own.

An alternative perspective, which is more consistent with the notion of a self-sufficient and omnibenevolent divinity, is that God created sentient beings in order for them to experience the joys and pleasures of life. On this view, humanity's purpose might be seen as living life to the fullest. God could then serve as a sort of exemplar for how this might be optimally accomplished. The advantage of this conception is neither God's goodness nor his perfection need be compromised. We must, however, be willing to follow the logical ramifications of this perspective. Namely, if we grant that God's creative inspiration was centered on the well-being of his creation, then it is not logically consistent for any creature to be permanently relegated to a place of eternal pain or suffering (i.e., hell). So while emulating God might be seen as important insofar as it contributes to personal happiness, the notion of God damning people to an eternal hell for a few years of unruly behavior is neither logical nor compatible with the notion of an omnibenevolent God. We must also contend with an even more difficult issue commonly known as "the problem of evil." The issue can be framed as follows: If God is all-loving, then he would want to maximize the happiness of its creation and to minimize, if not eliminate, its suffering (as depicted, for instance, in many conceptions of heaven[4]). But because pain and suffering appear to exist in rather large amounts, it follows that God is either indifferent to human suffering, thereby casting doubt on his goodness, or unable to prevent it, thereby questioning his power / omnipotence. For many INTPs and non-believers, there is no logically satisfying solution to the problem of evil, making it a detrimental blow to the tenability of theism.[5]

Despite the serious challenges associated with constructing a logically plausible argument for theism, there are still plenty of INTP theists in circulation (although, percentage wise, far fewer than we find among other personality types). One reason for this is that INTPs are going to believe what they want (or need) to believe. At times, their need to believe may be so powerful that all opposing arguments, however logical, will have little to no effect.

Moreover, some INTP theists may approach the issue of theism in an entirely different manner than I have, which may in turn lead them to different conclusions. They might argue, for instance, that beginning with questions like "Why would God create?" or "Why does so much evil exist?" is arbitrary and subjectively motivated, and that other starting points might be equally or more valid.[6]

It is also the case that INTPs' beliefs, religious or otherwise, reflect the respective needs and desires of their personality functions, especially the function(s) that currently wield the most control and influence. While we would typically expect Ti to have the strongest voice, this is not always the case, particularly in Phase II of INTPs' type development, which is characterized by a tug-of-war situation between their Ti and Fe. In times when their Fe has the upper hand, INTPs might be inclined to envision God as a perfect source of love. Or, they might imagine a day when the whole world is united under a single banner of mutual respect and understanding. These sorts of utopian ideals are clearly of Fe origin.

This prompts the question of whether we should criticize INTPs who permit their non-dominant functions to have a stronger voice in their beliefs and who therefore subscribe to a less than logical worldview. If such an INTP was arguing that his beliefs were objectively (as opposed to subjectively) valid, I would suggest that criticism is warranted. If, however, he were to admit that his views were subjectively orchestrated in order to meet his psychospiritual needs, it may be best to withhold criticism because his beliefs can be considered valid from an existential / pragmatic / psychospiritual standpoint. While an objectivist might argue that such an individual does himself no favors by comforting himself with illogical ideals, this overlooks the fact that not everyone is at a place in their life or development where they are capable of handling "the full truth" (assuming there is such a thing).[7]

Final Remarks

Generally speaking, INTPs think like philosophers. They are fiercely independent in their thinking and typically unwilling to turn off their minds in the name of blind faith. At the same time, they ultimately want many of the same things that religion promises, things like purpose, wisdom, and wholeness.[8] Therefore, INTPs who study philosophy should not be construed as seeking an arid, spiritless, or mechanical understanding of the world. The truth is they seek ideas that are both rationally satisfying and personally useful / meaningful. In the parlance of Ken Wilber, they strive to marry "sense and soul." In his book, *Jung's Four and Some Philosophers*, the self-declared INTP and professor of religion, Thomas King, offers us a glimpse into his own concern for sense and soul:

> "I have never had much interest in philosophy that does not include the soul of the philosopher, nor do I care for what is supposed to talk only of the soul. Rather, I am drawn to Socrates, Augustine, Teilhard, Kierkegaard, Jung and others as they tell of both the soul and objective being. In working with their texts, I have identified with them, and because of them know I am not standing alone."[9]

Notes

1. This brings up the question of whether INTPs gravitate more toward free will (i.e., unpredictability / freedom in the universe) or determinism. On the one hand, Einstein didn't want God playing dice (Ti), while on the other, he claimed that "the most beautiful thing we can experience is the mysterious" (Ne). In other words, INTPs want to believe in free will while at the same time expecting the universe to behave in relatively consistent and uniform

ways. In the end, the side they take will in large part depend on whether Ti or Ne gets the final word. Or, they may simply opt to remain agnostic on the matter.

2. If faith / fideism is the least preferred (or consciously preferred) epistemology for philosophers and INTPs, then we might associate faith with the feeling function, reasoning that they would be least comfortable relying on their "missing function." Moreover, of the four IN types, INFPs (F dominants) seem most inclined to invoke faith (C.S. Lewis is a good example), which further substantiates this observation. We could also correlate faith with sensing, since S types are more inclined to rely on faith and authority than N types. Based on this line of reasoning, we would expect NTs to use faith the least and SFs to employ it the most, which in my experience has generally held true. With that said, at some point in their lives, INTPs feel compelled to temper their rationalistic tendencies (see Chapter 14 for more on this), which may render them more open to the idea of a faith-based worldview. A number of brilliant philosophers, such as Pascal, Kierkegaard, and Wittgenstein, seemed surprisingly open to, or defensive of, faith. For more on faith as an epistemology, see the Standford Encyclopedia of Philosophy entry on fideism.

3. Of course, one could take a postmodernist or relativist position and claim that all ideas and methods are equal insofar as they are all social constructions. On this view, one might argue that philosophers or scientists are no closer to truth than anyone else. Most INTPs will ultimately reject this line of thought, even if largely for practical reasons. They find life more meaningful and enjoyable when they view truth as knowable, which includes seeing some ideas as better than others.

4. Although I can sympathize, to some extent, with the desire for immortality, the notion of eternal bliss, that is, of perfection in the afterlife, has never made good sense to me. If heaven is the ultimate goal, then why would God even bother to create a non-heavenly situation in the first place? In response to this question, believers often make some sort of argument for the importance of free will. But if everyone is made perfect in heaven, as many of believers argue, this would seem to require the elimination of free will, especially our freedom to sin. But this ensnares them in a logical trap. Either free will is part of their ideal reality, which means that heaven cannot be construed as a sinless place, or free will is not a part of their ideal reality, which makes it difficult to hold people liable for their earthly beliefs or actions. Whatever option they choose throws a wrench into the logical tenability of their usual storyline.

5. Many philosophers see the problem of evil as insurmountable and the strongest argument against the existence of a theistic God.

6. Kant, for instance, took a rather different approach to God and morality. From what I have gathered, he seemed to have been a theist (although some have fancied him a closet atheist). If Kant was indeed a theist, it might seem a bit perplexing considering the highly rational and, in many respects skeptical, nature of his entire philosophical program. To my knowledge, Kant didn't address the question of why God might have been compelled to create sentient beings in the first place. Rather, he started with the practical need for morality and, from there, reasoned that a moral standard or ideal (e.g., God) must exist. Kant focused less on the problem of evil than other thinkers, perhaps because he didn't consider human happiness to be the highest ideal. Kant's reluctance to speculate on abstract questions regarding God's nature or God's reasoning may have also stemmed from his prior conclusion that metaphysical speculation could provide us with real knowledge. If this was the case, we can at least respect Kant's concern for consistency, even if he failed to directly address some of the more interesting theological questions. We could also speculate that Kant started with a desire to believe in God in order to preserve a sense of meaning (Fe) regarding human existence. In her book, *Self and Subjectivity*, Kim Atkins writes, "It is said that Kant's aim, in setting out the conditions for and limitations of knowledge in the *Critique of Pure Reason*, was to limit reason to make room for faith."

7. We must exercise great discernment in these situations, recognizing that human beings are psychospiritually fragile and that *personal beliefs* do have a rightful place in the world. There are, however, two situations in which personal beliefs should be directly challenged. The first, which we've already touched on, is when dubious beliefs are being marketed as certain or objective truth. The second is when personal beliefs are apt to significantly harm others.

8. In my view, the best arguments for religion emphasize its potential value for enhancing our current earthly lives. For instance, the brilliant INTP philosopher-theologian Paul Tillich espoused that "religion is immediacy." I couldn't agree more. Adopting a postponement mentality (i.e., "I'm just waiting to go to heaven where all will be made right."), which is rooted in magical / escapist thinking, is a cop-out of the highest order. While not denying the potential benefits of envisioning a better future, a postponement mentality can lead to missed opportunities to grow and find meaning in the here and now. It may also inspire disconcern for, and poor stewardship of, our current resources—environmental, social, political, and otherwise. With that said, in cases where such a mentality proves innocuous, we must, in light of my remarks in Note 7, respect the individual's right to hold it.

9. King, T. *Jung's Four and Some Philosophers*. p. 311.

10

IRREDUCIBLE MIND

In the previous chapter, we explored reasons why INTPs are inclined to reject theism as a tenable worldview. However, we neglected to evaluate its opposite—atheism combined with scientific materialism (or simply "materialism")—to which we will now turn our attention. For it is often between the extremes of theism and materialism / atheism that INTPs discover their philosophical / religious "sweet spot."

Materialists see the world through mechanistic lenses. They envision the world, including humanity and its evolution, as a giant system or machine, one which is devoid of anything immaterial, such as mind or spirit. This lack of any uniquely human or spiritual element likely contributed to James' decision to label such thinkers tough-minded.

At minimum, INTPs' Ti can appreciate materialism's concern for logical consistency and order, as well as its interest in reducing things to their lowest common denominator. For instance, if there is no good reason to believe that what we call mind (or consciousness) is anything more than a by-product of complex arrangements of matter (e.g., brains), then we should applaud materialists for saying so.

With that said, my observations suggest that most INTPs are reluctant to wholeheartedly embrace materialism. A common reason for this is it detracts from their experience of life as meaningful (Fe) and mysterious (Ne). Viewing the world as a conglomeration of cold, lifeless, and predictable mechanisms is off-putting to both Ne and Fe. This makes it a rather uninspiring philosophy for the meaning-oriented INTP.

But is this really any different from the theist who believes for the sake of comfort, meaning, or inspiration? To the extent that both are informed by underlying psychological needs, I would concede a similarity (we might also note that materialists are influenced by their own set of psychological needs, e.g., those of S or Te). The difference is that many INTPs simply *cannot* believe in theism because of its perceived logical shortcomings. So rather than place all non-materialists in the same boat, we should consider whether there are non-theistic alternatives to materialism that might prove more logically satisfying to INTPs.

In *Beyond Good and Evil*, Nietzsche expressed his distaste for scientific materialism as well as its shortcomings as meaningful philosophy:

> "A 'scientific' interpretation of the world . . . might therefore still be one of the most stupid of all possible interpretations, meaning that it would be one of the poorest in meaning . . . An essentially mechanical world would be an essentially meaningless world. Assuming that one estimated the value of a piece of music according to how much of it could be counted, calculated, and expressed in formulas; how absurd would such a 'scientific' estimation of music be! What would one have comprehended, understood, grasped of it? Nothing, really nothing of what is 'music' in it!"[1]

Here, Nietzsche highlights his desire for a philosophy that is meaningful, and why he believes materialism falls short in this regard. To illustrate, he suggests that viewing a work of art, in this case a piece of music, purely in terms of mechanism (ST) will result in a forfeiture of what is most essential and valuable about it (i.e., its NF quality and meaning). For Nietzsche, the N and F elements must be honored and granted equal status in our view of reality. Of course, this is precisely what materialists are reluctant to do, preferring instead to reduce everything to ST parts and mechanisms.

Is Mind Reducible to Matter?

Underlying Nietzsche's argument is the sense that there is something special and unique about human experience / consciousness that cannot be reduced to, or explained in terms of, matter and mechanism. In other words, there is a qualititative character to our subjective experience that strikes us as distinctly different from that of physical reality. In short, we experience mind and matter as two different types of reality.

If we were to repeat Descartes' famous experiment, few would argue that we don't have subjective experience. I would argue that our subjective experience is the only thing we can know with absolute, first-hand certainty.[2] Even if the outside world proved to be nothing but an illusion or hallucination of the mind, the subjective experience itself cannot be doubted. As conveyed in his famous proclamation—"I think therefore I am."—Descartes concluded that thought was the most certain and fundamental reality. I would contend, however, that experience is even more fundamental than thought, since thought represents only one type of subjective experience. So when materialists argue that reality is nothing more than matter and mechanism, INTPs are forced to evaluate this in light of the one thing they know with certainty—their own subjective experience.

The critical question thus becomes: How likely is it that matter and mechanism can account for the qualitative character of our subjective experience? Put differently, can matter give rise to consciousness? It seems to me that INTPs have good reason to doubt that mind / consciousness / experience is fully reducible to matter and mechanism. Consider the views of Leibniz, Huxley, Nagel, and Jung on this issue:

Leibniz:

> "It must be confessed that perception and that which depends upon it are inexplicable on mechanical grounds, that is to say, by means of figures and motions."

Huxley:

> "How it is that anything so remarkable as a state of consciousness comes about as the result of irritating nervous tissue, is just as unaccountable as the appearance of the Djin when Aladdin rubbed his lamp."

Nagel:

> "If physicalism is to be defended, the phenomenological features must themselves be given a physical account. But when we examine their subjective character it seems that such a result is impossible."

Jung:

> "It is impossible to imagine how "experience" in the widest sense . . . can be made up exclusively of outer phenomenon. The psyche belongs to the very core of the mystery of life."

Of course, these sorts of arguments for what we might call the "unique nature" of consciousness are not unfamiliar to materialists, and they are always armed with rejoinders. One of their most common retorts is that human experience, or what is sometimes called "naïve experience," is not a reliable or viable tool for discerning truth. This argument is founded, at least in part, on the fact that humans have historically gotten many things wrong (e.g., geocentrism, the "flat earth" theory, etc.) when they place too much trust in their naïve experiences of the world. Materialists might cite how the historical march of science has been characterized by a consistent debunking of human myths, folk theories, and pseudoscience, as well as a replacement of those beliefs with scientific knowledge. Based on this impressive track record, they feel justified in asserting that science is epistemically superior to anything that can be known from naïve experience or introspection.

In response, the non-materialist might reply that just because human beings have gotten some things wrong does not prove that human subjectivity is characteristically unreliable. They might also point out that scientists rely heavily on their own subjectivity to guide their work. Indeed, philosophers and critics of science have long argued that science was conceived by, and continues to rely on, human minds. They thus see it as deeply ironic that, despite scientists' supposed distrust of subjectivity, their work remains inextricably rooted in it. They may accuse scientists of using their complex instruments and equations to distract themselves from one of the most fundamental features of reality—their own subjectivity.

I'd like to take a brief intermission here to point out that these disputes are largely rooted in Ti-Te differences. As we've seen, most philosophers are INTPs are therefore use Ti as their primary tool of inquiry. And because Ti is an introverted function, they spend a great deal of time immersed in their own minds, exploring their own subjective terrain. Consequently, the world of subjectivity feels very real, familiar, and trustworthy to them. Among other things, they trust that Ti can discern certain truths in an a priori fashion, that is, without the aid of external evidence. They therefore experience the mind as a unique sort of thing. By contrast, Te (and to some extent, Se) can be associated with science and materialism. Te employs an extraverted form of logic and is attuned to external facts and quantitative measures. Because it is outer-directed and constantly engaging with external objects, *it is less aware of its own subjective origins.* Therefore, Te users (i.e., TJs) and to some extent, ES types in general, are less apt to sympathize with the notion that the mind is a unique sort of thing. Moreover, because subjectivity cannot be experienced or apprehended from without, the only reality Te sees is one comprised of material structures and mechanisms. Considering these deep-seated Ti-Te differences, it is no surprise that these debates are often so polarized.

In addition to arguing from the historical march of science, materialists may cite other examples of the unreliability of human experience, such as how hallucinations fail to furnish an accurate picture of reality. But this argument misses the more fundamental point. The point is not whether hallucinations accurately reflect some outer reality. All that matters for the sake of this debate is that we all have subjective experience and that its nature is difficult, if not impossible, to explain in terms of matter and mechanism; we are only concerned with experience in its most basic sense—the subjective reality associated with being or existing.

Another common argument from materialists is that the mind is dependent on the brain and can therefore be seen as a mere by-product or "epiphenomenon" of complex arrangements of matter. In making this claim, they urge us to avoid the temptation to view consciousness as a special or unique sort of thing. But as is the case with so many things, *correlation does not prove causation*. While admitting a close relationship between mind and brain (i.e., the nature of the brain clearly affects our subjective experience), this does not prove that the brain is the ultimate source of our experience. Suggesting that brains give rise to minds is akin to arguing that televisions are the producers their programs. While it is obviously true that we cannot view programs without televisions (or similar devices), and that the type of television affects a program's presentation (e.g., its sound, appearance, etc.), it is equally true that programs are *not created* by televisions. We might therefore argue that the brain, while serving as a sort of shell or transmitter, does not create our subjective experience. This is why many INTPs prefer to see subjective experience as a fundamental feature of reality rather than an "emergent property" of matter.

The fundamentality of subjectivity is aptly expressed in INTP Ken Wilber's catchphrase—"every outer has inner." By this he means that all of reality not only has a physical form or appearance ("outer"), but also some sort of "inner" or subjective experience. In so doing, Wilber grants mind and matter equal ontological status, seeing them as inextricably co-occurrent; they represent different sides of the same coin. On this view, there are no disembodied gods or spirits, nor are there any entities without some of sort inner experience. Even the most rudimentary structures (e.g., atoms, molecules, etc.) are surmised to possess an interior or subjective element. Hence, whenever various physical structures (i.e., exteriors) join together in community, such as the human brain, so do their interiors.

The fact that we can more easily see or scientifically measure / manipulate exteriors (e.g., neurons) does not negate the reality of their correspondent interiors. If the interiority of things is mostly known and experienced from within, how can we reasonably expect to measure it from without? Similarly, if exteriors are best known from without, how can we expect to know them from within? So instead of trying to use the same tools to study interiors and exteriors, perhaps two different types of tools—introverted and extraverted—are required to understand the fundamental nature of things.

Panpsychism, Monism, & Pantheism

I would now like to introduce a few more concepts relating to the irreducibility of subjectivity. One such concept is panpsychism (a.k.a., panexperientialism), which *The Stanford Encyclopedia of Philosophy* defines as "the doctrine that mind is a fundamental feature of the world which exists throughout the universe." According to *Wikipedia*, "Panpsychism used to be the default theory in philosophy of mind, but it saw a decline during the 20th century with the rise of logical positivism. However, recent interest in the 'hard problem of consciousness' has once again made panpsychism a widespread theory." Panpsychism is closely related to notions such as monism, pantheism, immanence, and vitalism, all of which INTPs tend to be sympathetic to.

Monism is a quantitative concept. Simply put, it suggests that reality is one (e.g., "mono"), or is comprised of only one substance, rather than of more than one type of substance (as purported in dualism or pluralism).[3] Monism is commonly contrasted with dualism. Substance dualists do not see mind and matter as two sides of the same coin, but rather as two distinct substances that can exist independently of one another. This view is required, for instance, to posit the existence of disembodied spirits, deities, or souls. Hence, for the dualist, the fundamental nature of reality may look very different depending on where one happens to be looking.

In *Psychological Types*, Jung observed that "the monistic tendency is a characteristic of introversion." This makes sense when we consider that introverts attune to one primary thing—their own subjectivity. The interests and attention of extraverts, by contrast, are more diversified and widely distributed, which is why Jung links extraversion with pluralism. Whereas pluralists / extraverts seem largely content with a multiplicity of facts, details, or ideas, monists / introverts are more concerned with discerning underlying laws or essences. Introverted N types are particularly concerned with uncovering the core essence of things, with identifying the lowest common denominator.

Here's where things may get a little more confusing. Both materialists and pantheists can be classified as monists, since both see reality as ultimately one.[4] But unlike materialists, pantheists view reality as permeated by an immanent and irreducible mind.[5,6] And while they admit that reality exhibits different properties or attributes, most notably "mind and matter," pantheists see these as part of one and the same fundamental reality because they are always co-occurrent (i.e., every outer has an inner). For the same reason, pantheists are inclined to see both mind and matter as eternal. Mind didn't create matter, nor did matter create mind.

The essential philosophical groundwork for pantheism was laid by Spinoza (INTP) in his classic and most important work, *Ethics*, which has since been embraced and venerated by a number of great philosophers, many of whom were INTPs. Hegel (INTP), for instance, claimed that becoming a follower of Spinoza is "the commencement of all philosophy." Similarly, Deleuze (INTP) deemed Spinoza the "Christ" and "prince" of philosophy. Yet another INTP, Albert Einstein, proudly declared his belief in "Spinoza's God." Clearly, Spinoza's pantheism strikes a deep chord of resonance with INTPs.

From many INTPs, pantheism furnishes the optimal balance of elegance, meaning, mystery, and logical consistency / plausibility. It retains the specialness and irreducibility of mind, which can keep the door open to meaning and mystery, perhaps even mysticism. However, at least in its typical conception, pantheism contains no grand plan or purpose for humankind and is incompatible with special revelation. Rather, it conceives the universe as operating much like Ne: always changing and evolving, but with a certain blindness toward where it is headed. Pantheism can therefore be located somewhere in between materialism, which sees the universe as a giant machine, and theism, which sees God and reality through anthropomorphic lenses. Materialists, in turn, may dismiss pantheism as mystical or fanciful, while theists may consider it too impersonal or devoid of a satisfying purpose.

Notes

1. Nietzsche, F. *Beyond Good and Evil*. 1886.

2. Using the experience of subjectivity as an argument for the irreducibility of mind may seem to contradict my earlier suggestion about INTPs being rationalists (T) before empiricists (S). While I am open to this being an exception to that general rule, INTPs' inner experience might be seen as largely reflective of Ti and Ne, and therefore a different sort of thing than S empiricism. In philosophy, the term empiricism is typically used in an Se / Te sense. Moreover, philosophical consensus suggests that Descartes was a quintessential rationalist and my epistemic starting point is essentially the same as his.

3. My view of monism resembles that of "existence monism" or "substance monism." Layered atop this monism, however, is a "property dualism," which

suggests that despite the existence of only one essential thing or substance, we experience it as having two qualitatively distinct *properties*—mind and matter; hence, my use of the coin analogy.

4. If materialist monism (or what we've simply been calling materialism) is associated with introversion and Te, ISTJs would seem the most likely to subscribe to it (especially those raised in non-religious homes). We might associate pantheistic monism (or simply, pantheism) with introversion and intuition, particularly with Ne. Hence, INTPs and INFPs would seem the most apt to be pantheists, although INFP pantheism is apt to be more overtly mystical, as seen among proponents of psi phenomena, astrology, or New Age types of thinking.

5. The term "immanence" is also used to describe the Holy Spirit in Christianity. The pantheistic spirit is different, however, insofar as it is considered to be ubiquitous and non-discriminating with respect to an individual's particular religious beliefs.

6. Closely related to pantheism is the concept of "panentheism." While both conceive mind or spirit as immanent and ubiquitous, the panentheist also envisions the universe as possessing a consolidated spiritual center, almost like a soul or godhead. Interesting questions might emerge in exploring these perspectives: To what degree is everything spiritually interconnected? While we sense that we are spiritually connected within ourselves (e.g., the experience of being a singular or unified psychospiritual being), how, if at all, are we as individuals spiritually connected to everyone / everything else? Is there any basis for believing in psi phenomena?

11

LIFE & EVOLUTION

"The most beautiful thing we can experience is the
mysterious . . . It is enough for me to contemplate the mystery
of conscious life perpetuating itself through all eternity."
—*Albert Einstein*

As we've seen, INTPs are typically dissatisfied with the materialist worldview, preferring instead to see the universe as characteristically "alive." For this reason, they are often intrigued by the concepts of life and evolution.[1] Some may even take up studies in physiology or evolutionary biology. We should be careful, however, not to assume that INTPs' view of life is limited to the biological realm, since many will also think of it in a metaphysical sense, that is, as an expression and embodiment of an animating mind or spirit.

Among other things, INTPs are keen to explore the ways that life differs from non-life.[2] In thinking about this issue, they may observe that when a non-living thing, such as a wrist watch, is broken, it has no means of repairing itself. Without outside intervention, the watch will forever remain in a state of disrepair. Watches are also incapable of adapting themselves to unfavorable environments. If not waterproofed, for instance, they are unlikely to survive an accidental foray into the swimming pool or washing machine.

By contrast, life can repair itself (i.e., recover from an injury or illness), as well as adapt itself to myriad environments. It also entails a more complex and interesting type of inner experience, including a sense of whether it is healthy or ill. While a wristwatch has no notion of whether it's working or broken, an injured or diseased organism often knows when something is "wrong" (i.e., when there is a deviation from its inner standard of health or normalcy).

In striving to satisfy its own inner standards (e.g., health, homeostasis, developmental milestones, etc.), life can also be viewed as more purposeful and value-oriented than non-life. As the INTP historian Georges Canguilhem once remarked, "To live . . . is to prefer certain methods, circumstances, and directions to others. Life is the opposite of indifference."[3] Life's standards or preferences are conveyed by way of ideas, many of which are unconscious.[4] Through processes we don't fully understand, ideas (N) manage to guide and influence physiological processes (S).

Bergson: Life, Evolution, Freedom, & Creativity

INTPs are fascinated by the purposive nature of life, as well as the role of mind and ideas in its regulation and evolution. These themes are extensively explored in the works of one of my favorite INTP philosophers, the Frenchman Henri Bergson.[5]

Many know (and often criticize) Bergson as a "spiritualist" or "vitalist," the reasons for which will soon become evident. But Bergson is rarely dogmatic about his views and he should not be misconstrued as a starry-eyed idealist. I see him as characteristically sober and balanced in his presentation. He substantiates his points with strong Ti logic, as well as ample empirical evidence from the biological sciences.

Creative Evolution is one of Bergson's best and most famous works. Its prose is interesting and accessible, and its content empirically informed and conversant with both sides of the evolutionary debate (e.g., mechanism vs. vitalism).[6] I would now like to examine a few excerpts from the book that exemplify Bergson's intriguing perspectives on life and evolution. In this first excerpt, Bergson is reflecting on evolution as a whole, including the notion that life imbues matter with freedom and indeterminacy:

> "The role of life is to insert some indetermination into matter. Indeterminate, that is, unforeseeable, are the forms it creates in the course of its evolution. More and more indeterminate also, more and more free, is the activity to which these forms serve as the vehicle. A nervous system, with neurons placed end to end in such wise that, at the extremity of each, manifold ways open in which manifold questions present themselves, is a veritable reservoir of indetermination. That the main energy of the vital impulse [of life] has been spent in creating apparatus of this kind is, we believe, what a glance over the organized world as a whole easily shows."[7]

Here, Bergson cites the architecture of the nervous system, including its myriad synapses (which he sees as representing myriad possibilities), as evidence of life's impulse toward freedom. In contrast to purely mechanistic thinkers, Bergson does not see evolution as entirely accidental or as merely a passive response to environmental pressures. Rather, he believes, for reasons I will not fully enumerate here, that the vital impetus of life (i.e., the inner / mental / subjective element of reality) is characteristically free and creative, and therefore inspires the evolution of forms (e.g., complex nervous systems) that embody those traits. In taking what amounts to a pantheistic view of things, he sees mind and matter influencing each other at every turn, even in rudimentary organisms.

Bergson also characterizes life as moving in precisely the opposite direction of inert matter:

"Life is an effort to remount the inline that matter descends. This reveals to us the possibility, the necessity even, of a process the inverse of materiality."[8]

This can be seen as a reflection of Bergson's view that life / mind and matter constitute conceptual opposites, as well as his belief that the former is responsible for animating the latter.

Although Bergson repeatedly characterizes the life impulse as free, he does acknowledge (in my view, rightly) that the effects of this freedom are, to an important extent, limited and constrained by physical laws:

"If it were pure consciousness . . . it would be pure creative activity. In fact, however, it is riveted to an organism that subjects it to the general laws of inert matter. But everything happens as if it were doing its utmost to set itself free from these laws. The impetus of life, of which we are speaking, consists in a need of creation. It cannot create absolutely, because it is confronted with matter . . . But it seizes upon this matter . . . and strives to introduce the largest possible amount of indetermination and liberty."[9]

Why INTPs are Fascinated by Life, Mind, Spirit & Related Concepts

At various points in this book, we've touched on INTPs' love affair with concepts. In our last couple chapters, we've explored specific concepts—life, mind, and spirit—that INTPs are apt to find particularly interesting and meaningful. I would now like to consider why it is that INTPs are so enamored with these particular concepts.

As we've seen, Ne has a thirst for novelty, mystery, and creativity. And because INTPs see life / mind / spirit as the primary source of novelty, creativity, and indeterminacy in the universe, they are naturally intrigued by it. Moreover, because exploring these concepts is in many ways similar to studying Ne, it really amounts to studying themselves.

Put differently, these concepts exist at the interface of two of INTPs' most foundational interest areas—psychology and philosophy.

On a practical level, INTPs love exploring and synthesizing ideas. They rely on the creative acumen of Ne to keep their lives interesting and purposeful. This is another reason they enjoy contemplating concepts like life, mind, and spirit. Namely, if they value creativity and see life as inherently creative, then performing creative work can be viewed as an alignment with the creativity of life / spirit itself. This sort of imagery may imbue INTPs' creative efforts with a greater sense of meaning, mystery, and importance.

Fe also contributes to INTPs' interest in these concepts. Because INTPs have a relative paucity of feeling in their lives, philosophizing about NF things like life or spirit (as opposed to ST things like matter and mechanism) can help them feel more whole and integrated.

Finally, some INTPs (e.g., Bergson, Hegel, Wilber) have opted to conceive mind / spirit not only as an immanent and creative force, but also as a sort of goal or ideal toward which all life is striving and evolving.[10] For Bergson, the arrow of evolution pointed toward greater freedom, since spirit itself is characteristically free. Others, such as Teilhard de Chardin, have viewed evolution as a progression toward greater consciousness (e.g., the "Omega Point"), a process which has been described in terms of "spirit becoming aware of its own nature through human beings." It is easy to see why INTPs might be drawn to these sorts of conceptions, which imbue human life and its evolution with a greater sense of meaning and purpose.

Notes

1. In addition to evolution, INTPs are often intrigued by life processes such as "self-organization" and "emergence," both of which involve the emergence of intelligent systems that supersede the intelligence of their constituent parts. A good example is the ant colony. Despite being comprised of what, on their own, appear to be relatively "dumb ants," ant colonies are surprisingly sophisticated and intelligent systems. The same could be said of the human

brain, which relies on clusters of neurons which, considered independently, aren't terribly smart. There are three basic ways of explaining these sorts of emergent phenomena. The first option involves positing a God that carefully designed these intelligent systems, akin to how a human being designs a watch. Another view, often held by scientists, is that the answer lies in some yet to be discovered mechanism in the parts themselves, such as a chemical signal or sensory apparatus that allows ants to coordinate themselves in intelligent ways. While INTPs are sympathetic to the notion that the seeds of intelligence must somehow reside in the parts of these systems, INTPs may be more open than scientists to the possibility that the intelligence may be arising from unseen mental / subjective factors; this constitutes our third option. On this view, when a group of ants gather in proximity, their colonizing intelligence is thought to emerge from interactions among their minds, similar to how the human mind emerges from the interactions of the individual minds contained within (or associated with) each of its neurons.

2. If one accepts the pantheistic viewpoint, he must also acknowledge that the seeds of life (i.e., the inner / subjective element) are present in inorganic matter as well. But what we typically call the "origin of life" depended on the emergence of arrangements of matter that were more conducive and responsive to these seeds. This further supports Bergson's observation that mind is not all powerful. Rather, the degree to which it can express itself is to some extent limited by the physical shell it inhabits. Perhaps we will discover ways of further freeing the mind from physical restraints through technology, bioengineering, or mental disciplines such as meditation.

3. Delaporte, F. A Vital Rationalist: Selected Writings from Georges Canguilhem. p. 72.

4. Since we know from depth psychology, as well as from various phenomena such as the "ideomotor effect," that ideas can exert their effects outside of conscious awareness, it is not unreasonable to suggest that ideas play a guiding role in even the most rudimentary life forms.

5. It is unfortunate that the initial excitement spawned by Bergson's work was rather short-lived, eclipsed by early 20th-century interest in existentialism and phenomenology. More recently, one of Bergson's greatest admirers and proponents, Gilles Deleuze, has rekindled some interest in Bergsonian thought.

6. In biological / evolutionary circles, vitalism (or finalism) and mechanism are typically viewed as constituting opposite ends of the theoretical spectrum. While there is no universal doctrine of vitalism, our discussions in this and the previous chapter offer a basic sense of how vitalists might view life and its evolution.

7. Bergson, H. *Creative Evolution*. p. 83.

8. Ibid. p. 163.

9. Ibid. p. 163, 167. Both Bergson and Spinoza were INTPs, yet Bergson emphasized freedom and Spinoza was a determinist (Einstein seemed to lean toward determinism as well). Can these two views be reconciled? To a large extent, I think they can be. In his classic work, Ethics, Spinoza basically argued that because the nature of mind (or God) is consistent, its effects will necessarily and predictably be in accord with its nature. At the same time, we must acknowledge that there are myriad factors that interact and combine in any complex system. This can make it difficult to predict outcomes with absolute certainty. We might therefore see creativity and free will as convenient terms for describing the relative unpredictability of complex systems. So even if Spinoza's determinism ultimately proved correct on an ontological level, our experience of unpredictability (and choice) compels us to function as though free will exists. See Chapter 9, Note 1 for more on how INTPs might approach the free will vs. determinism issue.

10. Enstating spirit as the goal of evolution amounts to a sort of "teleological pantheism." In order for such a philosophy to have any religious, moral, or practical import, one must ascribe certain qualities or virtues to spirit. Indeed, one of the reasons I've struggled with teleological perspectives is I find it difficult to make such attributions with any degree of confidence. I am inclined to join Bergson and Whitehead in viewing life / mind / spirit as creative, and perhaps to a certain extent wise, intuitive, or intelligent. However, if Jung is correct in asserting that reality is comprised of opposites, how can we in good faith say that spirit is characterized by x (e.g., good), but not y (e.g., evil)? If it is true that spirit is comprised of more or less equal measures of opposing forces, it seems inappropriate to classify the notion of "evolution advancing toward spirit" as utopian. Of course, one could opt to take a dualistic stance and make the case for the existence of two distinct types of spirit (e.g., good and evil). But as we've seen, dualism is typically less attractive to INTPs since it is less parsimonious and, to the INTP mind, less plausible. Hence, INTPs who are drawn to a teleological view of evolution are more apt to argue that, while spirit may seem to be comprised of opposing forces, this is only because it is imprisoned in matter, which prevents us from consistently witnessing its true nature. Bergson, as well as many Eastern thinkers, seemed to think along these lines. One might also argue that opposites are somehow reconciled in spirit, as they are in psychological integration, which allows spirit to be characterized as "good." On this view, the most prominent or important attribute of spirit would be *unity*.

12

PHILOSOPHICAL TYPES

Most philosophers or students of philosophy eventually notice that they enjoy more intellectual camaraderie with some philosophers than they do with others. Likewise, a philosopher's "circle of friends" can often be discerned by perusing his in-line citations and bibliography. Even apart from citations, students of philosophy will detect similarities in style, method, and content among like-minded philosophers.

In my view, these philosophical similarities and kinships are best understood through the lens of personality type. Of course, I am by no means the first to make this observation. In *Psychological Types*, Jung analyzes the works of numerous thinkers and philosophers from the perspective of type. But even prior to Jung, other thinkers, most notably William James, had proffered astute observations along these lines. Consider this candid and insightful passage from James' book, *Pragmatism*:

> "The history of philosophy is, to a great extent, that of a certain clash of human temperaments . . . Of whatever temperament a philosopher is, he tries, when philosophizing, to sink the fact of his temperament . . . Yet his temperament really gives him a stronger bias than any of his more strictly objective premises. It loads the evidence for him one way or

the other . . . He trusts his temperament. Wanting a universe that suits it, he believes in any representation of the universe that does suit it . . . Yet in the forum he can make no claim, on bare ground of his temperament, to superior discernment or authority. There arises thus a certain insincerity in our philosophic discussions; the potentest of all our premises is never mentioned."[1]

James goes on to describe two primary philosophical types, which he called "tender-minded" and "tough-minded."

The Tender-Minded Type

Rationalistic (proceeding by "principles")
Intellectualistic
Idealistic
Optimistic
Religious
Free-willist[2]
Monistic
Dogmatic[3]

The Tough-Minded Type

Empirical (proceeding by "facts")
Sensationalistic
Materialistic
Pessimistic
Irreligious
Fatalistic
Pluralistic
Skeptical

From where I sit, James got a surprising number of things right in the above breakdown (even Jung agreed with much of it).[4] With certain exceptions, I see INTPs as generally fitting nicely into the tender-minded camp (Jung also associated James' tender-minded camp with the introverted thinker). Philosophers such as Hegel, Fichte, and Bergson are apt representatives of this camp, while thinkers like Hobbes, Hume, Russell, and Carnap epitomize the tough-minded type.

James' breakdown is valuable because it demonstrates how certain philosophical propensities are interrelated and tend to occur together. This of course comes as no surprise to the typologist, who is inclined to view philosophical types as superficial manifestations of underlying type differences. In other words, the typologist is apt to view personality type as more foundational. The same holds for type and political preferences, which I touched on in *The INTP*.

The Continental & Analytic Traditions

We can also associate James' tender-minded type with what is commonly called the *continental* school of philosophy, and his tough-minded type with the *analytic* school. This continental-analytic delineation is best viewed as an informal typology (there is no actual continental or analytic school), similar to that of James, which offers a convenient snapshot of a thinker's philosophical bent. In my view, the continental-analytical distinction does a great job of highlighting core philosophical differences, which of course ultimately stem from type differences.

Continental philosophy finds its roots in French and German thought, with the term *continent* referring to that of Europe. Generally speaking, continentalists are drawn to subjectivity, history, idealism, introspection, ethics, and speculative thinking. We might even invoke Pirsig here and suggest they are concerned with *qualitative* philosophy. They tend to be less enthusiastic toward, and more apt to criticize, science and logical positivism. Thinkers in this camp are usually NP types, most commonly NTPs.

The analytic school is typically associated with certain British or American thinkers. It is closely allied with, and defensive of, science and its methods. Typologically, the analytic school can be associated with the Extraverted Sensing and Thinking, including a preference for empiricism (Se), induction, and standardized methods (Te). In his book, *The Age of Analysis*, philosopher Morton White offers a thumbnail sketch of the analytic philosopher:

> "Analysts are all hostile to speculative and obscurely written metaphysics [i.e., to Ti methods] of the kind one finds in the later works of Whitehead, to the kind of writing we see in Bergson and Husserl . . . Analysts think of philosophy not as a rival to science but rather as an activity partly devoted to clarifying it. They are relatively unconcerned with advancing moral philosophy and are more interested in finding out what is meant by words . . ."[5]

As White points out, analytic philosophers are inclined to see continentalists as overly vague and speculative, and therefore contributing little of real substance to the advancement of knowledge. Continentalists, in turn, may criticize analytic philosophers for their relative inattention to the underlying assumptions of their work (i.e., their lack of clear Ti foundations), as well as for avoidance of issues that matter most to human beings (e.g., ethics, religion, existential issues, etc.).

Notes

1. James, W. *Pragmatism*. p. 7.

2. Of James' eight tender-minded characteristics, INTPs may be most apt to question the "free-willist" and "dogmatic" descriptors. Having already discussed the free will vs. determinism issue in previous footnotes, I will simply remind readers that Ne will always rally for free will. Moreover, as

subjectively-oriented introverts, INTPs naturally see the mind as a unique type of thing, one which is not bound by the same laws and restrictions as matter. By contrast, the tough-minded type, in being oriented to external objects by way of Te or Se, is less attuned to, as well as less enamored with, the experience of his own subjectivity.

3. I realize that James' "dogmatic" descriptor may seem a bit confusing, particularly in light of how I used the term in this book's introduction. I think James chose the term because of its relationship to "proceeding by principles." Namely, if one leads with principles (Ti), he is more apt to dismiss, ignore, or downplay external facts or evidence. And in this respect, he might be seen as acting dogmatically. Noam Chomsky is a good example of a principled / dogmatic INTP, particularly in his later years.

4. Although I think James may have seen himself as transcending the tender / tough-minded dichotomy, I would classify him as more tender-minded. Both ENTPs and INTPs tend to lean this direction (see Chapter 3, Note 3 for my discussion of James' probable status as an ENTP).

5. White, M. *The Age of Analysis*. p. 190.

13

PHILOSOPHICAL PATHS

As we've seen, INTPs love to explore ideas pertaining to religion and metaphysics.[1,2] While contemplating metaphysical ideas can certainly be a rewarding and informative enterprise (Heidegger once declared that "philosophy is metaphysics"), there are a number of other branches of philosophy INTPs may find appealing—history, the philosophy of science, phenomenology, existentialism, critical theory, and pragmatism. We will explore each of these in this chapter including why, from a type perspective, INTPs might take interest in them. We will also discuss how these subdisciplines are interrelated and come together within the continental school of philosophy.

History

Interest in historical studies can be roughly associated with the Ne-Si function pair, which is why NPs and SJs (i.e., Ne and Si users) are the types most commonly intrigued by history. Ne is a characteristically fluid and open-ended function. It views things as emerging from a complex web of factors and is reluctant to grant any single factor a greater causal role than another. It is egalitarian, perhaps even agnostic, with respect to causation. It sees too many factors at play to establish clear lines of causation. These characteristics are well-suited to the study of history, which is typically a non-reductive and explorative enterprise. While history certainly entails plenty of concrete facts and details (Si), historians (especially NP historians) mostly enjoy the process of seeing and interpreting historical connections (Ne) rather than simply learning new facts.

As we've seen, Si can be associated with retrospection. It sees the past as a repository of valuable information that can guide or inform one's actions. INTPs may therefore see history as an interesting and valid lens for understanding human beings and the evolution of their ideas. Because Si is lower in their functional stack, we might expect INTPs' interest in history to emerge later in life, after trying their hand at metaphysics and other forms of armchair speculation (Ti-Ne). Interestingly, this is also how things seem to have unfolded in the history of philosophy, with metaphysics enjoying favor from the time of ancient Greece up until the Enlightenment. Following the Enlightenment, metaphysical and religious claims were viewed with increasing skepticism. This allowed empiricism (S), both scientific and historical, to emerge as the ruling epistemology, especially in Britain and the U.S.

For quite some time, I failed to understand why INTPs would take a strong interest in history. I could understand wanting to see the big picture of things (Ne), but the thought of wading through infinite facts and details was frankly repelling to me. I am not alone in this, knowing other INTPs who prefer reflecting on metaphysical concepts rather than historical or contingent ones. I eventually realized, however, that INTP history buffs aren't really interested in what we might call "S history" (i.e., trivial historical details), at least not for its own sake. Rather, they are interested in "N history," that is, the history and evolution of human ideas (i.e., intellectual history). For the N historian, contextual details are only important insofar as they are relevant to the evolution of ideas.

A good example of an N historian is the INTP historian of science, Georges Canguilhem, who came to be known by some as the "vital rationalist" (an apropos INTP moniker). My first encounter with

Canguilhem was through his book, *The Normal and the Pathological*. One thing that stood out to me was his focus on the historical exploration of *concepts*. To that point, I had wrongly assumed that history was mostly about dates and details, not about ideas and concepts. But here was a historian who loved what I loved— concepts. As one of Canguilhem's expositors, Hans-Jorg Rheinberger, observed:

> "Canguilhem has a clear predilection for a history of concepts, a history of problems meandering through the historical space of the sciences. While he talks about scientific objects, it is mainly concepts which he addresses . . . Canguilhem was a master of conceptual landscape painting."[3]

I see INTP historians operating much like INTP self-seekers. Both seek understanding through exploring webs of concepts and experiences over time. INTP self-seekers strive to understand their lives in light of the concepts and experiences that have been important to them. Likewise, INTPs historians peruse historical concepts and contexts that they find personally interesting or important. In the words of Canguilhem: "The historian of science has no choice but to define his object. It is his decision alone (Ti) that determines the interest and importance of his subject matter."[4]

We can now see why INTPs might be drawn to historical study, especially that which allows them to engage their interests in people (Fe) and concepts (Ti-Ne). Moreover, historians typically maintain that all their conclusions are tentative, which ensures there will always be more for them to explore. Canguilhem points out, for instance, that history constantly needs to be reconceived because new developments in current thought provide new lenses for interpreting and evaluating the past:

> "It is the epistemologist who is called to furnish history with the principle of judgment by teaching it the most recent language spoken . . . and in thus permitting it to retreat into

the past, back to the time when this language ceases to be intelligible or translatable . . ."[5]

While most INTPs have a knack for being fair and balanced in their work, this seems particularly true of INTP historians, scholars, and expositors, who tend to be more patient, less impulsive, and arguably further along in their type development. While surely a minority among INTPs, they are worthy of respect, admiration, and perhaps even emulation.

Existentialism

Existentialism emerged largely as a response to post-Enlightenment rationalism, secularism, and nihilism. Responding to Nietzsche's now famous (or infamous) "God is dead" proclamation, the existentialists took it as their task to explore ways in which individuals could discover or create meaning apart from organized religion. The values and meaning that had historically been furnished by religion would somehow need to be discerned and cultivated by the individual himself. Similar to the romanticists and transcendentalists, many existentialists were looking to restore spirit, mostly in an experiential (rather than theological) sense, in an increasingly secular landscape. In using the term *secular*, I am not suggesting that everyone had suddenly become atheists. What I mean, and what Nietzsche and others intended, was that traditional religion, as well as theism in general, had lost much of its traction among intellectuals. This produced a vacuum of existential meaning and purpose, one which the existentialists, romanticists, and others attempted to remedy.

On the whole, existentialists were not interested in science, metaphysics, or history. The locus of their concerns was not external but internal. Their primary objective was to understand the subjective experiences and concerns of the individual. In this sense, existentialism was more explicitly concrete in its focus than other types of philosophy. While philosophers had historically taken interest in both metaphysical and existential issues, the existentialists essentially bracketed metaphysics in order to focus exclusively on the existential predicament of the individual. Of course, this overlooks the fact that for some individuals, especially INTPs, metaphysical exploration can play an important role in their existential well-being.

The existentialists, romanticists, and transcendentalists also brought an experimental attitude to life. Consider, for example, Thoreau's famous life experiment at Walden Pond. Others, such as Albert Camus and Jean Paul Sartre, experimented with different modes of living and being through their novels. Nietzsche tinkered with ascetic practices in hopes of augmenting the intensity and meaningfulness of his subjective experience. What all of these thinkers had in common was a desire to make their lives more intense, interesting, or meaningful. In some respects they can be seen as trying to reengineer the power and meaning associated with the religious experience, but without invoking God or religion.

Taken as a whole, existentialist thought might be viewed as an exploration of the potentials and powers of the individual to cultivate a richer and fuller life. Its influence is still with us today, as exemplified in mottos such as "follow your bliss," "be yourself," or "do what you love."

Typologically, existentialism (and romanticism) is probably best characterized as an FP / Fi (and Ne) enterprise (Camus, Kierkegaard, Thoreau, and Rousseau may all have been INFPs[6]; Sartre was an INTJ and therefore also had Fi). One exception is Martin Heidegger who was certainly a T type, perhaps even an INTP. Heidegger was more classically philosophical than the other existentialists with respect to his concern for metaphysics and ontology. We might say that Heidegger brought a philosopher's mind to existential topics, whereas the FP existentialists were more poetic and feeling-oriented in their approach.

Despite the Fi leanings of many existentialist writers, INTPs nonetheless feel a sense of kinship with existentialists' predominant concern of cultivating more authentic, meaningful, and purposeful lives. According to thinkers like Nietzsche and Kierkegaard, life is better when one embraces and commits to something (e.g., a purpose) rather than remaining in a perpetual state of ambivalence or skepticism. These sorts of notions can be inspiring to INTPs, granting them the "permission" and moral support they need to wholemindedly believe in something. Moreover, as champions of subjectivity, existentialists afford the individual complete autonomy in fashioning his beliefs, which serves as another point of attraction for INTPs.

Critical Theory

Critical theory is in many respects a continuation and application of the work of Kant. Its chief concern is epistemological in nature. Among other things, critical theorists are concerned with the underlying motivations or "interests" of knowledge producers and knowledge-producing disciplines. They believe that truth claims can only be properly understood and contextualized if a discipline's (or individual's) motivating interests have been lain bare. Jurgen Habermaas has suggested, for instance, that science is motivated by an interest in "technical control." From his vantage point, this casts doubt on the common notion that science's primary concern is the discovery of objective truth.

In some respects, critical theory resembles typology in its concern for exposing and clarifying the subjective foundations of human thought. Both might also be viewed as attempting to "level the playing field" with regard to the tenability of various epistemologies. The typologist, for instance, might emphasize how T, N, S, and F all have a rightful place in our knowledge economy. Similarly, the critical theorist might argue that scientists have no greater access to, or interest in, truth than philosophers. They simply have different core biases and motivations.

It is not difficult to see why INTPs might be drawn to critical theory; INTPs are always concerned with foundational knowledge (Ti), especially that pertaining to human motivations (Fe). They also value the preservation of ample intellectual space for wide-ranging ideational explorations, including metaphysical ones. And as long as science and empiricism continue to rule the epistemological roost, doing so will remain an uphill battle. They may therefore feel compelled to don their critical caps as a means of defending intellectual freedom and diversity.

Phenomenology

Phenomenology is really just a fancy word for the study of the human mind through careful and controlled introspection. It was founded by the German philosopher and INTP, Edmund Husserl.

One feature of phenomenology (or introspection in general) that invariably appeals to INTPs is its non-reductive approach to consciousness. Namely, phenomenology doesn't try to "explain away" consciousness or deem it a mere by-product of the brain. Rather, it approaches it on its own terms as it subjectively manifests.

Phenomenology might also serve as a sort of back door to metaphysics. Namely, if we broaden our definition of empiricism to include subjective experience, then experiences shown to be universal might be used as evidence for the ontological fundamentality of mind or consciousness. We employed this sort of approach in our discussion of the irreducibility of mind in Chapter 10.

Phenomenology also has great potential for practical application. Namely, if we can inwardly study and understand the workings of the mind through introspection, we might also discover ways of recalibrating our minds in order to optimize our experience. Of course, monks and mystics have been doing this for millennia, and there is plenty to be learned from their experiences and insights.

Applied psychologists such as Mihalyi Csikszentmihaly are also incorporating certain phenomenological insights in their work.

Despite its numerous points of attraction, some INTPs may struggle to get on the phenomenological bandwagon because of its relative disconnectedness from culture and history. Phenomenological experiments, such as those outlined by Husserl, have a rather structured and isolated feel to them. This may be off-putting to INTPs who desire more interpersonal or cultural touchpoints in the philosophical journey.

Pragmatism

Pragmatism was founded by Charles Sanders Peirce and was further developed and advocated by William James and John Dewey. According to *Wikipedia* (2016):

> "Pragmatism rejects the idea that the function of thought is to describe, represent, or mirror reality. Instead, pragmatists consider thought an instrument or tool for prediction, problem solving and action. Pragmatists contend that most philosophical topics—such as the nature of knowledge, language, concepts, meaning, belief, and science—are best viewed in terms of their practical uses and successes. The philosophy of pragmatism emphasizes the practical application of ideas by acting on them to test them in human experiences."

As we've seen, INTPs can generally be seen as pragmatic in their approach to life and work, employing myriad hacks and workarounds to "make things work." Moreover, insofar as they use philosophy as a means to an end (i.e., a means to a better life), they can be seen as operating pragmatically.

When it comes to adopting pragmatism as a philosophy, INTPs will differ in the degree to which they insist that an idea must *represent reality* (i.e., constitute truth in the traditional sense) in order to be considered valuable (as opposed to being pragmatically valuable). But even those who appreciate the pragmatist approach may conclude that it falls short as an inspirational and meaningful philosophy, which may compel them to invest the majority of their philosophical resources elsewhere.

Eastern Philosophy

The rational emphasis of the Western philosophic tradition is commonly juxtaposed with the more holistic approach of the East. Of the personality types, NPs, including INTPs, seem most naturally drawn to Eastern thought. INTPs often appreciate the pantheistic worldview of many Eastern traditions, as seen, for instance, in Buddhism or Taoism. They may also see Eastern philosophy as more compatible with reason and contemporary knowledge than Western religions. Furthermore, INTPs may take interest in the phenomenology, as well as the pragmatic benefits, of certain Eastern practices, such as yoga and meditation.

With that said, INTPs may struggle with the East's relative disinterest in logic and concepts. So unless INTPs can find satisfying ways of exploring Eastern thought on a conceptual plane, their level of interest may fail to extend beyond the cursory.

Continentialism

All of the above branches of philosophy, with the exception Eastern philosophy and to some extent pragmatism,[7] can be roughly associated with the continental philosophic tradition. But what is it, we might ask, that connects them?

Habermaas has suggested that the foundational interest of the philosopher (by which I suspect he has in mind the continental philosopher) is *emancipation*. In using this term, Habermaas is not referring to emancipation or freedom in the political sense, but in the psychological sense. In other words, he sees the philosopher as having a profound concern for freedom of thought. Of course, this is not at all surprising when we consider Ti's need for autonomy and Ne's thirst for unfettered exploration. Philosophers' penchant for polyvalent concepts also speaks to their need for ideational versatility and freedom.

Another common concern among the continentalist disciplines is exploring and understanding the human, subjective, or qualitative element of reality, and to do so in a holistic, non-reductive way: philosophical historians study the evolution of human ideas, critical theorists examine subjective biases and motivations, existentialists explore the challenges of the human condition, phenomenologists inquire into the nature of human subjectivity and consciousness, and pragmatists approach truth in terms of its practical benefits for human beings. The continentalist interest in holistically exploring the human element helps us understand why philosophy is typically coupled with the humanities rather than the sciences.

As discussed in the previous chapter, analytic philosophers are less holistic in their approach. Staunch proponents of objectivity, they strive to eliminate or control for the subjective element to the greatest extent possible. Instead of allowing Ti to approach an issue in the way it sees fit, they rely on standardized and quantitative methods (Te). They also feel that morality, ethics, and other "soft" issues are not the philosopher's concern. In their view, intermixing ethics (i.e., "what should be") with philosophical analysis (i.e., "what is") is a methodological mistake of the highest order.

Notes

1. In today's post-modern philosophical climate, many academic philosophers see metaphysics as little more than a philosophical relic. With the exception

of basic introductory courses, metaphysics has been effectively jettisoned by many American philosophy departments. One of the best-known contemporary academic proponents of metaphysics and the irreducibility of consciousness is the Australian philosopher David Chalmers. The American philosopher Thomas Nagel also takes a non-reductive view of consciousness. While not an academic, Ken Wilber has played an important role in keeping the metaphysical spirit alive for laypersons. Wilber has devoted ample space to explaining why academics have forsaken metaphysics, and why they may be missing the mark in doing so. Unfortunately, Wilber's enthusiastic embrace of Buddhist mysticism, as well as his somewhat uncritical adoption and promotion of certain developmental frameworks, has not improved his standing among academics. If you are interested in reading Wilber, I recommend starting with his first book, *The Spectrum of Consciousness*, or his more extensive masterpiece, *Sex, Ecology, Spirituality*.

2. Surprisingly, metaphysics has enjoyed a bit of a recent renaissance in some analytic philosophy departments. While this is certainly a good thing in my view, the metaphysical approaches taken by analytic philosophers are often dualistic / Platonic and may therefore be less compelling for INTPs. If you recall from Chapter 10, INTPs gravitate more toward monism.

3. Gutting, G. *Continental Philosophy of Science*. p. 193.

4. Delaport, F. *A Vital Rationalist: Selected Writings from Georges Canguilhem*. p. 28.

5. Canguilhem, G. "The Object of the History of the Sciences."

6. Most type enthusiasts consider Kierkegaard an INFP because of his lyrical style, melancholy demeanor, propensity for sentimentalism, and rejection of philosophical rationalism. However, there are parts of his work, such as his book *Either / Or* and the opening portion of his *Concluding Unscientific Postscript*, that suggest he might be an INTP. In *Either / Or*, Kierkegaard proffers thoughts and observations on how to live well, many of which look a lot like Ti principles and disciplines. In addition to his advice to abstain from marriage and close friendships, he suggests: "One ought to devote oneself to pleasure with a certain suspicion, a certain wariness . . . One should keep the enjoyment under control, never spreading every sail to the wind . . ." He also espouses the "principle of limitation: the more you limit yourself, the more fertile you become in invention." In my view, it is easier to envision an INTP fashioning these sorts of ideas than an INFP. These and other facets of Kierkegaard's work led Thomas King, author of *Jung's Four and Some Philosophers*, to type Kierkegaard as an INTP. If in fact he was an INTP, we would need to attribute his F expressions to an inferior Fe (as opposed to a dominant Fi if he were an INFP). This is one of the trickier aspects of typing,

that is, determining whether an individual's presentation is stemming from the dominant function or from a compensatory response of a non-dominant function (Jung touches on this difficulty in *Psychological Types*).

7. Pragmatism is sometimes viewed as bridging the continental and analytic schools.

PART IV

Toward Integration

14

"NOTHING MORE TO EXPLORE"

In *What is Philosophy?*, Deleuze and Guattari suggest that one of the central problems of philosophy is "to acquire consistency without losing the infinite into which thought plunges." This notion of "the infinite" dovetails nicely with Jurgen Habermaas's remark, discussed in the previous chapter, regarding the philosopher's concern for ideational freedom. Namely, philosophers (and INTPs) don't merely strive for logical consistency, but also for opportunities to explore novel ideas and possibilities. This tension can be conceptually framed in numerous ways: Ti vs. Ne, order vs. chaos, planned vs. spontaneous, predictable vs. novel, "left brain" vs. "right brain," and so on. In his book, Immanence, Miguel de Beistegui nicely summarizes this tension:

> "Thought must learn to move freely and effortlessly between
> the sphere of pure chaos, in which all things originate, but
> which also harbors the danger of madness, and the sphere
> of fully individuated substances, facts, and states of affairs,
> which harbors the danger of ossification and listlessness."[1]

When functioning in extreme Ne mode, such as pursuing countless rabbit trails of ideas, INTPs may eventually reach the end of their tolerance for ideational chaos. As de Beistegui points out, too much disorder "harbors the danger of madness." This level of disorder can prove unsettling for INTPs, particularly with respect to their Ti's need for structure and order. But *too much* structure can also present problems for INTPs. When Ti is operating dictatorially, INTPs may become obsessed with categorizing, structuring, or consolidating ideas, which may ultimately dispose them to a sense of "ossification or listlessness."

A related challenge posed by Ti is its propensity to attribute meaning and importance to a relatively narrow range of interests or activities. Like a magnet, it constantly draws INTPs back toward its primary concerns. For instance, an INTP philosopher who decides to venture out and explore politics may struggle if his Ti declares that political ideas are less foundational, and therefore less important, than philosophical ones. For such INTPs, it can seem inordinately difficult to stretch or extend Ti's tether.

INTPs are also notorious for losing interest in a topic once they believe they have understood its basic essence or structure. In such instances, Ti, particularly its left-brained element, essentially declares, "There is nothing more to explore here." This can occur on both small and large scales. With regard to the former, INTPs might skim an article, conclude that they have understood its general point, and then move onto something else. While such small-scale judgments are typically innocuous (some might even call them "efficient"), larger-scale ones may be more debilitating. If an INTP were to conclude, for example, that he is no longer interested in his chosen career field because he has already explored all that is worth knowing, then he has a significant problem on his hands.

Moreover, INTPs are routinely drawn to grand explanatory theories (e.g., meta-theories, "theories of everything"). The prospect of finding a sweeping, once-and-for-all conception of reality can be deeply enticing to them. Naturally enamored with universal laws and patterns, INTPs are prone to assume that the patterns observed at higher levels of complexity will also exist at lower levels, and vice-versa. In other words, they expect to find the same essential patterns at play at all levels of reality (e.g., fractals). The problem is, once INTPs put the finishing touches on their own superordinate theory of reality, they may feel there is nothing left for them to do. They may lack the motivation to work on other types of theories because of their belief that grand theories are the only important ones. Operating deductively, they assume that all of reality can be ultimately explained in terms of a handful of general laws, making "middle-range" theories of lesser interest to them.

In time, the confluence of the above propensities can culminate in two things: a more crystallized worldview and a relative diminishment of intellectual fervor and curiosity. As the INTP's worldview starts to coalesce and crystallize over time, life can start to seem more predictable and less novel. We can associate these changes with increasing influence of the left cerebral hemisphere, or what is colloquially called the "left brain." In his masterpiece, *The Master and His Emissary*, Iain McGilchrist writes, "The left hemisphere deals with what it already knows . . . the world it has made for itself . . . and therefore prioritizes the expected—its process is predictive."[2] As life begins to feel more predictable and ideas less novel, INTPs can become increasingly unsettled when the "nothing more to explore" thought surfaces more frequently or becomes harder for them to dismiss or ignore. Indeed, it is one of the more frightening and distressing thoughts INTPs can have. Since much of their livelihood is founded on exploring new ideas and possibilities (Ne), the obviation and cessation of those explorations would constitute an existential blow of colossal proportions.

Tempering the Left Hemisphere

To combat the "nothing more to explore" problem and restore a sense of meaning, interest, and novelty in their lives, INTPs feel compelled to find ways of dealing with a left hemisphere that has come to feel increasingly oppressive. One approach they invariably consider is simply cutting it off—a veritable act of *sacrificium intellectus*.

The idea here is that if rational thinking led to the development of a crystallized worldview that now feels oppressive, then maybe the solution is to jettison rationality altogether. Perhaps life will be more interesting and meaningful without the structured worldview of the left hemisphere. As part of this experiment, INTPs may try to supplant their typical rational endeavors with right-brained activities such as poetry, fiction writing, music, design, painting, etc. in hopes of revitalizing their lives.

The demotion of rationality, along with the pursuit of novelty and unfettered creativity, is a central theme in the works of Deleuze. Deleuze can often be found rallying against excessive structure (i.e., against his own Ti proclivities) and championing the pursuit of novel ideas and experiences ("the infinite"). He even goes as far as idealizing the schizophrenic state, one characterized by unalloyed feeling and imagining. According to Deleuze, schizophrenia is a "harrowing, emotionally overwhelming experience, which brings the individual as close as possible to matter, to a burning, living center of matter."

Kierkegaard also viewed excessive rationality, particularly that of grand philosophical systems, as inimical. One of his favorite targets was Hegel, whose work epitomized what he detested most in philosophy. Kierkegaard deplored the fact that Hegel's sweeping theory left little room for individuality, novelty, and personal freedom, making it a dire threat to the psychospiritual livelihood of the individual.

Kierkegaard was not merely a critic, however. As an existentialist, he was driven to find solutions to the "nothing more to explore" problem. Among other things, Kierkegaard saw self-imposed limits and disciplines as critical to keeping life fresh and interesting. In *Either / Or*, he cites the example of a prisoner in solitary confinement who finds great fascination in observing the activities of a spider. Noting that "even the most insignificant things may accidentally offer rich material for amusement," Kierkegaard felt that learning to appreciate life's simple pleasures was critical to the well-lived life. But in order to be open and responsive to such pleasures, one must first develop the appropriate mindset. According to Kierkegaard, this mindset is developed, ironically, by way of limits and strictures. After all, had the prisoner not been confined, he may have never found such great delight in the frolics of a spider. Thus, one must subject oneself to self-engineered rules and disciplines in order to prepare the mind to appreciate life's subtleties.

Kierkegaard also espoused the art of *forgetting*, or what might be better termed selective *forgetting*. He discovered that the value and meaningfulness of one's experience could be enhanced by intentionally forgetting (i.e., barring from consciousness) certain thoughts or memories. For instance, an adult might benefit from periodically suspending his beliefs and identity to make way for an attitude of childlike wonder and curiosity. Similarly, INTPs might find it useful to temporarily "forget" their universal theories in order to appreciate certain problems or ideas on their own terms. An INTP pantheist, for example, will naturally tend to see things through a pantheistic lens. But what might happen, when investigating something new, if he were to suspend this belief? Suddenly, he would no longer be looking to confirm or bolster what he already believes (i.e., no longer leading with a J bias or agenda), but would have opened himself to new possibilities (Ne) and empirical evidence (S). No longer beholden to broad generalities and presuppositions, he would be free to explore and evaluate the issue on its own terms. In so doing, his approach would shift from deduction toward induction, from rationalism toward empiricism, from judging toward perceiving.[3] By temporarily "forgetting" his universal theory, particular issues and phenomena can be explored on their own terms. According to McGilchrist, Wittgenstein preferred this sort of approach:

> "One of his [Wittgenstein's] favorite sayings was 'Everything is what it is and not another thing,' an expression of the right hemisphere's commitment to the sheer quiddity of each individual thing . . . and its resistance to the reductionism inevitable in the system building of the left hemisphere."[4]

Deleuze, Kierkegaard, and Wittgenstein all recognized the psychospiritual dangers of adopting grand, universal theories. Wittgenstein once remarked, for instance, that scientific accounts "leave us with the distinct impression that everything has been accounted for; they give us the illusion of explaining a world that we might do better to wonder at." Each of these thinkers sensed that the solution to the "nothing more to explore" problem must involve some measure of shift away from universals in order to pave the way for greater appreciation of the particulars of life. Once one has embraced a universal theory, he experiences a sense of closure, the sense that there is nothing left to be done. But because the number of particulars in the world is infinite, they can serve as a consistent source of novelty and interest.

Typologically, this sort of reasoning coincides with INTPs' development of Si, that is, when they no longer feel satisfied operating exclusively as universal theorists (Ti-Ne). This developmental shift helps explain why philosophers' views often change over time, sometimes dramatically (e.g., the "early" Wittgenstein vs. the "late" Wittgenstein). Namely, their views and methods change because their existential situation demands it. In times of psychospiritual crisis, there is often a sense of "change or die," which leaves one little choice but to heed the demands of the psyche.

In sum, Deleuze, Kierkegaard, and Wittgenstein all sought ways of sidestepping the static and stifling worldview offered by left hemisphere in order to preserve a spirit of openness, novelty, and freedom.[5] It was out of similar concern that I made the case in Chapter 8 for an approach that can furnish INTPs with greater philosophical freedom. Neuropsychologically, these efforts can be seen as efforts to remain engaged and connected with the right hemisphere—the hemisphere of novelty. As McGilchrist observed:

> "In almost every case, what is new must first be present in the right hemisphere . . . The right hemisphere alone attends to the peripheral field of vision from which new experience

tends to come; only the right hemisphere can direct attention to the edges of our awareness . . . Novel experience induces changes in the right hippocampus, but not the left. So it is no surprise that phenomenologically the right hemisphere is attuned to the apprehension of anything new . . . It is more capable of a frame shift . . . and is especially important for flexibility of thought . . ."[6]

INTPs also strive to maintain a sense of wonder and mystery in their lives. Plato held that the mark of the philosopher is a "sense of wonder." Aristotle asserted that "it is owing to their wonder that men . . . philosophize." Wittgenstein espoused that "man has to awaken again to wonder." Einstein saw mystery as the most beautiful of life's experiences. Like novelty, McGilchrist associates mystery and wonder with the right hemisphere. He also suggests that there is a natural dialogue that transpires between the two hemispheres:

"The routine of daily life, in which things have their familiar place and order, can dull things into what Heidegger called inauthenticity . . . Its left hemispheric representation comes to take the place of the thing itself (broadly, the idea of a hammer replaces the thing as it is experienced). However . . . when the hammer becomes the focus of my attention, it becomes possible to rediscover the authenticity that had been lost, because the detachment enables us to see it anew as an existing thing, something remarkable, almost with a sense of wonder."[7]

This interhemispheric tension is ever-present for INTPs. In many respects, they thrive on it. They are constantly formulating theories and ideas, while simultaneously trying to avoid feeling confined or stifled by them. They have a consistent appetite for both order (left hemisphere / Ti) and novelty / freedom (right hemisphere / Ne). While one might suspect that the concurrence of these opposing tendencies would foster constant problems, it is only when one hemisphere (or function) becomes excessively dominant that things become problematic. For reasons we've discussed, an over-active left hemisphere is the more common culprit for INTPs, especially later in life. In the previous quote, McGilchrist, in concert with Heidegger, touches on an intriguing way of reengaging the right hemisphere and restoring a sense of interest and wonder. However, we must postpone further discussion of this matter until Chapter 16.

"It's Already Been Done Before"

INTPs may also struggle with the "It's already been done before" notion, which speaks to their concern that other capable people have already accomplished the important work in their interest area. Consider the following INTP blog comment:

> "I am a good writer. However anything I might write about is covered elsewhere, most often by people who are far more knowledgeable than I. Thus, I am of the opinion that anything I'd add would merely be more 'digital noise,' and I don't write to 'hear myself speak.' Thus, I find no strong draw or passion to write."

This comment highlights some real and pervasive concerns among INTPs. One is their concern that their work will be redundant or will simply add more extraverted "noise" to the already over-populated world of ideas. INTPs may also feel that the only important ideas are the foundational ones, and that those ideas have already been explored by some of the world's greatest minds. When we examine these concerns more closely, we discover that they are largely extraverted in nature. Namely, they are centered on social comparisons (e.g., "someone more knowledgeable than I") and extraverted reasoning (e.g., "someone's already done that before"). They are also marked by a sense of closure (J) and resignation, the sense that "there is nothing new under the sun." Our question then, is whether INTPs can find ways of circumventing or undercutting these concerns.

At the broadest level, we might consider whether novelty and creativity are realities in our universe. If it is true that things change over time and that new forms emerge, then novelty and creativity would seem to be features of reality. And if INTPs are part of this ever-changing reality, there should, in theory, always be new things for them to explore and create. Of course, INTPs might retort by asserting that novelty and creativity aren't sufficient on their own, but must be associated with important or foundational ideas. In reply, I might suggest that there are plenty of unexplored connections between foundational ideas, as well as myriad opportunities for exploration pertaining to foundational ideas. So even if the INTP isn't the originator of a foundational idea, there is still an infinite number of original ways he can create with or around that idea, similar to how musicians are constantly creating new combinations of notes and sounds. Here we must remember that a fundamental part of INTPs' purpose, as is true for all NP types, is to explore and create (Ne). So while INTPs may emphasize the importance of foundational ideas (Ti), they also need to grant their Ne sufficient freedom to roam and to scope out new connections and associations; if Ti comprises the roots and trunk of the INTP's tree, Ne (and Si) grows and develops its branches.

It can also be easy for negative left-brain messages to gain a foothold if INTPs don't have contradicting evidence at the ready. For instance, it can be useful for INTPs to recall instances when they discovered something new or meaningful when they weren't expecting it, thereby demonstrating that life does in fact have more interesting things in store for them. Taking up a creative craft, such as writing, may also prove useful in this regard, allowing INTPs to be routinely surprised by the unexpected and novel gifts that emerge through the creative process.

Finally, INTPs can combat the "it's already been done before" notion by emphasizing the *intrinsic enjoyment* that comes from their work, rather than focusing on external results or making social comparisons. Those who can successfully shift their locus of value inwardly and learn to appreciate the process of their work (see Chapter 16), will find themselves more consistently satisfied. If INTPs can recognize, with Pirsig and Kierkegaard, that what matters most is the quality of their subjective experience (this is particularly true for IP types), then they will have made an important first step toward a more satisfying life.

Final Remarks

In this chapter, we have explored how increasing left-hemisphere influence, including its superordinate theories, crystallized worldview, and negative messages (e.g., "nothing more to explore"), can have the unwanted effect of rendering life less novel, interesting, and meaningful for INTPs. This requires the development of an antidote, that is, an approach that restores a more optimal balance between the two hemispheres. This may include intentionally "forgetting" or suspending certain beliefs or theories to carve out more imaginative space for the right hemisphere. In so doing, INTPs are in some respects contravening the ideational certainty they worked hard to secure as seekers. This should not be taken to mean that their seeking efforts were for naught, but simply demonstrates that both sides of the brain, as well as all four functions, must always be sufficiently engaged and integrated. When operating as seekers, INTPs can be seen as perceiving (P) in order to achieve a certain goal (J), such as the clarification of their purpose and worldview. But once their purpose and worldview have crystallized, they start to feel as though the J / left-brained element has amassed too much power. This compels them to develop and employ strategies, such as those discussed in this chapter, to restore the optimal J-P / hemispheric balance.

Lastly, it is hard not to comment on how ironic it must appear when INTPs feel compelled to turn against their long-standing romance with rationalism. As we saw in Chapter 3, rationalism is an epistemology that comes rather naturally to INTPs, but when their rationalistic worldview starts to feel psychospiritually oppressive or stagnating, "something's got to give." To temper or counterbalance their rationalistic propensities, INTPs will at some point consider it necessary to explore philosophical alternatives such as existentialism, historicism, empiricism, or post-modernism. Other may turn to religion or spirituality. These alternatives furnish INTPs with opportunities to develop and integrate their non-dominant functions. This is not to say, of course, that INTPs will (or should) reject rationalism altogether. What they are seeking is the right balance, one in which reason (Ti) is paired with enough openness and curiosity (Ne) to keep life feeling fresh, interesting, and meaningful.

Notes

1. de Beistegui, M. *Immanence*. p. 71.

2. McGilchrist, I. *The Master and His Emissary*. p. 40.

3. This should not be seen as an entirely new approach for INTPs. After all, when operating as seekers, INTPs are in consistent dialogue with the particulars (e.g., experimenting with particular ideas and possibilities). It is only once their worldview has become more crystallized that their approach takes on a more deductive or dogmatic flavor.

4. McGilchrist, I. *The Master and His Emissary*. p. 157.

5. We might also view Kant's most famous and influential work, *Critique of Pure Reason*, as an attempt to place limits on rationality. According to philosopher Kim Atkins, "It is said that Kant's aim, in setting out the conditions for and limitations of knowledge in the *Critique of Pure Reason* , was to limit reason to make room for faith." Kant may have been seeking, even if unwittingly, to counterbalance his clearly potent Ti with his inferior Fe's desire for faith and meaning.

6. McGilchrist, I. *The Master and His Emissary*. p. 40.

7. Ibid. p. 154.

15

THE TRANSITION

As children, we are animated by dreams and ideals, inhabiting a world where nearly anything seems possible. However, with time and experience, our childhood ideals slowly give way to a more sober and realistic worldview. While this is a normal feature of human development, it can have the disappointing effect of rendering life less magical and more predictable. Once we finally experience much anticipated events such as attending college or getting married, our sense of intrigue and excitement drops, often to disquietingly low levels. Likewise, many people spend much of their adult lives anticipating the "golden years" of retirement, a time when they hope to relax and enjoy themselves. But they are often surprised and unsettled when they discover that, instead of being golden, retirement has left them feeling listless and apathetic toward life.

INTPs who have finally committed themselves to a purpose may encounter similar challenges. After years of searching and anticipation, they may experience a dramatic let down once they identify their purpose. This is at once surprising and disappointing, as they expected that finding their purpose would augment, rather than diminish, their energy and motivation. Like retirees, they may feel confused and shorted when their new reality is a far cry from what they had envisioned. Consequently, many INTPs will resist or recoil from this new reality. Some may even go as far as rejecting their newfound purpose in hopes of returning to the halcyon days of seekerhood.

More specifically, INTPs transitioning out of seekerhood are concerned that their diminished sense of energy and motivation will make it impossible for them to effectively enact their purpose.[1] They struggle to see how they can be productive, let alone produce high-quality work, without higher levels of drive and inspiration. A looming sense of disenchantment is also common for such INTPs, as life has come to seem less magical and more predictable; the "nothing more to explore" problem is one manifestation of this. From a developmental perspective, these changes often occur near the end of the differentiation phase of type development (Phase II). As Jung observed:

> "Since the aims of the second half of life are different from those of the first, to linger too long in the youthful attitude means a division of the will. Consciousness still presses forward . . . but the unconscious lags behind because the strength and the inner will-power needed for further expansion has been sapped. This lack of unity with oneself begets discontent."[2]

These changes make it increasingly difficult for INTPs to stay positive, hopeful, and actively engaged in life. At some point, INTPs come to a point of decision in which they can either give up and succumb to nihilism, or try to remain hopeful and seek out solutions.

Our key question then, is how INTPs can effectively transition from the phase of life characterized by incessant seeking (including purpose seeking), the pursuit of lofty ideals, and differentiation (i.e., Phase II) into the final phase of their development (Phase III), which is marked by integration and the enactment of their life's purpose.

Because purposeful work is central to their psychospiritual wellness, the way forward for INTPs must include *constructive action pertaining to their purpose.* INTPs are typically at their best when they are investing in constructive and meaningful work, which is why finding a purpose is felt to be imperative in the first place. But here again we are confronted with our aforementioned problem, involving a perceived shortage of energy and motivation to carry out their purpose. With life's big dreams behind them, INTPs worry that there may be nothing left to inspire them. Having seen through many of life's myths and illusions, the world looks very different—less magical, less enchanting, less pregnant with possibility—than it once did.

This sort of stripped-down, demythologized world has comprised the starting point for many existentialist writers. In their view, once one experiences the world as impotent with respect to the provision of meaning, he must set out to cultivate his own meaning and purpose. But how is this to be accomplished? How can INTPs find meaning and be productive when life no longer feels magical, when they can no longer rely on lofty ideals to pull them forward?

The Rational & The Spiritual

In attempting to resolve their existential difficulties, INTPs may turn to spirituality for potential solutions. Since integration comes after differentiation and is commonly considered a "higher" stage of development, it is often associated or conflated with spirituality. Hence, INTPs may conclude that, having differentiated themselves and discovered their purpose, spirituality is the next step in their developmental sequence.

Unfortunately, as INTPs go about dabbling in spiritual literature and practices, they often sense that something isn't quite right. Namely, it feels as though they've suddenly leapt from a life characterized by self-definition and rational thought to its diametric opposite, one that seems largely unconcerned with individuality and rationality. Not only does this introduce a troubling sense of discontinuity with respect to their life story, but it also seems to devalue all the time, effort, and discoveries associated with their differentiation. In other words, if spirituality has little use for rationality and individuality, INTPs may feel that all their efforts as seekers were for naught. And if this is the case, they may wonder why differentiation was even necessary in the first place.

As we saw in our Chapter 8 discussion of the religious versus typological approach to wisdom, there is a tendency for people to take an either-or approach, heralding either religion / spirituality or psychology / typology as the key to wise living. So when INTPs start investigating spirituality, they may feel they've been transported to a world that is disconnected from the world of rationality. And unless they can find a satisfying way of connecting these two worlds— the spiritual and the rational—they will continue to feel that their existential difficulties haven't been sufficiently resolved.

Here one might argue that theology or metaphysics could provide the bridge between spirituality and rationality that INTPs are seeking. To some extent this is true, and many INTPs take this path, especially in the first half of life. But we must recall that this chapter is largely focused on INTPs who have either lost faith in, or are no longer energized by, big ideals, including those associated with religion or metaphysics; we might describe this variety of INTP as *post-idealist*.[3] For them, theology or metaphysics cannot, in and of itself, furnish the remedy they are seeking.

With that said, even INTPs who have abandoned theology or are agnostic toward God's existence may nonetheless sense that religion / spirituality contains at least a kernel of truth. And perhaps that kernel, whatever it turns out to be, might somehow help them see their way out of their existential predicament. In my view, this is a reasonable hypothesis, especially when one considers the abundance of evidence from developmental psychology substantiating the existence of a phase of human development that comes after differentiation, which many psychologists have described in terms of *integration, unity,* or wholeness. And when these sorts of descriptors are being employed, it is hard not to imagine a type of experience that resembles what we mean when we use the word spiritual.

Perhaps the most important thing that spiritual studies or practices can furnish INTPs is an alternative approach to life, and especially their work. At first blush, it may seem unusual to emphasize the way in which spirituality might enhance one's work. But for INTPs, life is largely about their work and the fleshing-out of their purpose. So if spirituality fails to supply INTPs with work-related wisdom, it will remain, at best, a matter of secondary importance.

What type of approach then, can spirituality offer INTPs in order to assuage their existential concerns and supply them with the meaning and energy they need to effectively enact their purpose? In my view, a *present-oriented mindset,* as emphasized in many Eastern spiritual traditions, is apt to be most helpful for INTPs. While this notion may seem rather simple, perhaps even a bit cliché, its merits are long-established in Eastern cultures. It has also garnered substantial attention and support from Western psychologists in the last couple decades. In the next chapter, we will unpack this approach and its relationship to integration.

Notes

1. Not all INTPs will experience a let-down after identifying their purpose. For instance, those who find their purpose early in life (e.g., Einstein, Gates) may experience little to no let-down whatsoever, since so much of their lives are still ahead of them. The same may be true of those who, after identifying their purpose, continue to be driven by ambition or external rewards (Fe). Despite these inconsistencies, it is nonetheless the case that all INTPs will experience existential let-downs or crises at some point in their adult lives. Some crises will be centered on inadequate differentiation (e.g., one who suddenly realizes at mid-life that he has been living a prescribed, rather than authentic, life), while others stem from the completion of differentiation (e.g., the discovery of one's purpose) or from the loss of meaningful ideals over time. Moreover, I recognize that differentiation (e.g., honing one's talents / craft) will continue after the discovery of one's purpose. Strictly speaking, one could argue that

differentiation is transpiring at every moment of life. Regardless, here is what is most important for our purposes: 1) A certain amount of differentiation must occur prior to integration. 2) The differentiation phase is marked by existential crises, some of which may only be resolved through integration.

2. Jung, CJ. *Psychological Reflections*. p. 108.

3. In using the term *post-idealist*, I am not referring to philosophical idealism, but to a more general form of idealism (i.e., pursuing and being energized by big ideals). Moreover, I am not suggesting that post-idealist INTPs have in any way retired from exploring ideas or concepts. They simply find themselves in a situation where they are no longer driven by ideals because, as Colin Wilson put it, "they see too deep and too much." Having seen through the illusions associated with self-related, religious, and other ideals, they are no longer inspired by them, at least not in the way they once were. They have for the most part jettisoned their "rose-colored glasses" and become more sober (although not necessarily pessimistic or cynical) in their outlook.

16

INTEGRATION

Most INTPs don't seek integration for its own sake. The notion of "being whole" is rarely a primary motivator for them, at least not consciously. More commonly, INTPs move toward integration *out of practical necessity*. Having reached a place of post-idealism, they are in many respects forced to reengineer their approach to life and work; their happiness and well-being depend upon it.

In the previous chapter, I suggested that INTPs seek an approach that will furnish them with meaning and energy, as well as help them effectively flesh-out their purpose, and do so without the aid of lofty ideals. In this chapter, we will explore such an approach. We will also discuss the nature of integration, as well as strategies INTPs can employ to cultivate and routinely experience integration in their work.

The Problem Provides (Part of) the Solution

As INTPs progress in their quest, they develop a clearer understanding of the world and themselves, including seeing through the myths and illusions they encounter along the way. This may entail the loss of religious beliefs, romantic ideals, self-related illusions, and ideals pertaining to the value of money, achievement, or fame. In short, INTPs come to see themselves and the world *more realistically.*

The evolution of INTPs' understanding is largely characterized by a process of *stripping away.* Among the most significant things pruned from their understanding are the illusions and negative elements associated with the ego.[1] In coming to see themselves more clearly, INTPs become more aware of their personal shortcomings, including the darker elements of their personality. When this is combined with knowledge of the relative impotence of worldly success with respect to their personal happiness, they discover what proves to be a most important virtue for them—*humility.*

More specifically, INTPs learn the sobering but valuable lesson that they are not nearly as important to the world as they might have imagined. Once they grasp the full implications of this realization, it can change them in profound ways. Among other things, they no longer fancy themselves as saviors of humanity (Fe). While relinquishing this sort of grandiose ideal is not always easy, once INTPs manage to do so, they experience a great sense of relief and liberation. With the fate of the world no longer riding on their shoulders, they are free to focus on the *intrinsic value* of their work, which can take them a long way in resolving their I-E struggles. Namely, once their extraverted fantasies have faded (especially the grandiose ones), it becomes far easier for them to discern and embrace their authentic, introverted interests. They can also start taking themselves and their work a little less seriously, which can further dissolve self-imposed pressures and increase their sense of freedom.

Another important virtue INTPs come to develop is *patience.* In many cases, their discovery of patience coincides with the identification of their purpose. Once they settle on a purpose, their sense of urgency diminishes, as it no longer seems necessary for them to continue frantically seeking. Another patience-enhancing factor is the shrinking of their ego.[2] As their ego diminishes, INTPs feel less compelled to prove or promote themselves to others, thereby allowing them to bring a more patient attitude to their life and work.

Interestingly, INTPs often don't intentionally set out to become more humble or patient. As you may recall from Chapter 5, they naturally orient themselves to energy rather than moral duty or piety. Hence, the development of these virtues might be seen as largely spawned by time itself. The title of this section, "The Problem Provides (Part of) the Solution," points to the fact that time, which eventuates substantial losses of ideals and energy, also furnishes part of the remedy to this problem through the diminishment of the ego and the development of certain core virtues. And while these changes are not entirely sufficient to resolve INTPs' foremost existential concerns, they pave the way for a more comprehensive solution, which we will now discuss.

Present / Presence Orientation

When operating as seekers, INTPs derive the lion's share of their energy from the pursuit of future rewards and ideals. For post-idealist INTPs, this "carrot on a stick" method has become less effective, which behooves them to find another way of securing the energy and meaning required to successfully enact their purpose. As mentioned in the previous chapter, a present-orientation can prove surprisingly useful in this respect.

When INTPs redirect their gaze from the future to the present, they become privy to a new type of experience. Like a future-directed gaze, a present-orientation infuses their experience with meaning and energy, but it does so in a *subtler way*. Although this experience is typically less intense and adrenalized than that furnished by an idealized future-orientation, it can nonetheless supply INTPs with the energy and meaning they need to consistently find satisfaction in their lives and work.

The energy and meaning supplied by a present-orientation is derived from Being itself.[3,4] The subtle, yet powerful experience of Being, or what Heidegger referred to as *presence*, can only fully manifest itself when one is attuned to what is happening in the present moment. Adopting a present or presence-orientation allows INTPs to be more aware of their own bodily experiences (e.g., feelings, sensations), more sensitive to the environment (e.g., the prisoner's amusement with the spider), and more authentically engaged with others. When their minds is not caught up in dreaming or worrying about the future (or the past), mental resources can be harnessed to furnish a richer experience of whatever is happening in the present moment. Thus, a spider no longer needs to be "just another spider" (i.e., a detached, left-hemisphere objectification), but can comprise part of unique and novel experience in a particular moment and context.

From a typological angle, a present-orientation keeps INTPs grounded to the concrete elements (SF) of life rather than operating like disembodied minds (NT). In making this point, I am not advocating for the elimination of the NT element, which would ultimately prove unsatisfying to the INTP, but am simply arguing for the value of keeping the NT element connected to SF particulars. One might of think of it as a straddling of the line between the abstract and the concrete, or between the top (Ti and Ne) and bottom (Si and Fe) halves of the functional stack. With respect to the functional stack, INTPs will ultimately find their "center" between Ne, which can be roughly associated with the mind, as well as a future-orientation, and Si, which can be associated with the physical body, as well as a past-orientation. By marrying the abstract and concrete, as well as the future and past, in the present moment, INTPs can more fully experience, understand, and appreciate Being itself, which is synonymous with their typological integration. One could also argue that it grants them greater access to wisdom insofar as *wisdom* is associated with integration and insight into the nature of Being.

INTPs can also benefit from attending to the *historical present*, that is, to contemporary collective affairs. Rather than focusing only on past, future, or eternal truths, they can work to understand and influence the world around them. This may include participating in local affairs, which is more concrete and contextualized than say, theorizing about global trends. By applying their NT abilities in the context of their local community or workplace, INTPs are apt to feel more integrated and connected to others. With that said, working on collective issues (Fe) may prove somewhat less satisfying for INTPs who have yet to fully differentiate. Many INTPs feel they must first discover who they are as individuals before they can authentically invest themselves in collective affairs. For instance, Bill Gates needed to discover and execute his purpose as an innovator and entrepreneur before he could authentically devote himself to philanthropic endeavors (Fe).

Process Mindset

Another related and important concept for INTPs is that of being *process-oriented*. Rather than fixating on goals or outcomes, process-oriented individuals strive to savor and learn from the process of their work. INTPs can better understand the nature of the process mindset by observing dominant perceiving types (i.e., EPs and IJs), such as ENP journalists, who in many respects embody this sort of approach. I've always been impressed by the fact that ENP journalists seem perfectly content to discuss nearly anything that comes their way. Rather than leading with an agenda, as an IP (or EJ) type might be inclined to do, they simply track whatever is happening around them. They don't wed themselves to any particular type of content, but are committed to a process (i.e., reporting).

With that said, we must be careful that we aren't simply exchanging one extreme for another. Since INTPs lead with an introverted judging function (Ti), they will naturally have more circumscribed interests than ENPs. What ENPs can offer is a picture of where INTPs are headed in their type development. Namely, as INTPs advance in their development, they learn to temper their judging (Ti) and spend more time perceiving (Ne and Si) and orienting themselves to the process of their work.[5] They will therefore display, in increasing measure, the process mindset that comes rather naturally to the Ne-dominant ENP.

In developing a process mindset, INTPs are apt to become less particular and more dispassionate with respect to the content of their work. This is due to the fact that the process (and Being) itself supplies them with ample meaning and energy. This has the fortunate effect of lengthening Ti's tether and thereby serving to combat the "nothing more to explore" problem.

The acclaimed INTP historian of philosophy, Frederick Copleston, embodied a process approach, as illustrated in the following portrait of Copleston:

> "He did not give himself away at all easily, and this was as true of his intellectual as of his religious attitudes. For example, his mammoth History is marked at all times . . . by an enviable objectivity, and by his willingness to be fair and to let the facts speak for themselves . . . Copleston keeps his cards very close to his chest, with the result that it is exceedingly difficult to discover where his own judgments lay . . . This self-imposed reticence made for great clarity and objectivity in his treatment of philosophers as diverse as Plotinus and Hume; but it was never altogether clear whether the reserve resulted from the desire not to let history become the victim of ideology, or because he had no point of view from which he wrote."[6]

As highlighted in this vignette, Copleston approached his work with a high level of dispassion. Rather than showcasing his personal opinions, he exhibited a loyalty to the process of his work as a historian. Having read several of Copleston's books, I can say that his ability to approach every philosopher, even those of an opposing mindset, with a similar level of concern and objectivity, was truly remarkable. Moreover, instead of writing a one-time, sweeping history of philosophy, as an INTP might be tempted to do, he exercised great patience and discipline (Si), investigating shorter periods of philosophical history in a more thorough and detailed fashion. This allowed him to make his purpose a lifetime vocation, rather than a one-time project. And it is this sort of sustained investment that INTPs ultimately want.

What many don't understand, however, is exactly how to get to that point. They assume that the key lies in selecting the right craft or interest area, but what they may fail to see or develop is *the type of mindset* required for them to operate in a sustainable and effective manner. Having developed the optimal mindset, I would argue that Copleston could have enjoyed a similar measure of success and satisfaction in other lines of work. In other words, it was the way he approached his work, more than anything else, that made him special and worthy of emulation. In this respect, we can appreciate Pirsig's quip: "Want to know how to paint a perfect painting? Make yourself perfect then paint naturally." This is what a process mindset offers INTPs, a chance to simultaneously better themselves and their work.

But how does this square with our prior discussions regarding the importance of INTPs clarifying their personal beliefs? Does emphasizing *the how*, rather than *the what* element of their work, obviate the need for them to pin-down their personal beliefs and interests?

Here, we must recall the importance of thinking along developmental lines. Namely, we must remember that INTPs undergo differentiation (i.e., move away from neutrality and toward a specific identity) before integration. Consequently, Phase II INTPs feel compelled to clarify their beliefs, interests, and purpose before they are willing or capable of fully embracing a process approach a la Copleston.[7] For them, whittling down the content (J) of their purpose takes precedence over process (P).

Flow

We will now turn our attention to a related concept, that of *flow*, which was coined by the esteemed psychologist Mihalyi Csikszentmihaly. Flow states are characterized by a sense of deep absorption in an activity. Individuals immersed in flow tend to forget about themselves and their personal concerns. Notions such as "losing track of time" and "being in the zone" are closely related to the flow experience.

In order to experience or "find flow," the activity must provide the right amount of challenge and stimulation. If it is too difficult, anxiety or frustration is apt to arise. If it is too easy, boredom may ensue. Typologically, flow is more likely to occur when all four functions are meaningfully engaged, especially the dominant and auxiliary function.

According to Csikszentmihaly, flow is the optimal type of human experience. One reason we appreciate flow is its association with mental focus. Research has shown that we are predictably less happy when our minds wander and one of the best antidotes is mental focus. As happiness researcher Matt Killingsworth reports:

> "People's minds wander a lot. Forty-seven percent of the time, people are thinking about something other than what they're currently doing . . . When our minds wander, we often think about unpleasant things: our worries, our anxieties, our regrets . . . We found that people are substantially less happy when their minds are wandering than when they're not, which is unfortunate considering we do it so often. Moreover, the size of this effect is large—how often a person's mind wanders, and what they think about when it does, is far more predictive of happiness than how much money they make, for example."[8]

To maximize the quality of their work, as well as the quality of their experience while working, INTPs must find ways of routinely experiencing flow. In addition to its association with mental focus, flow enhances creativity and goes hand-in-hand with a process mindset, which helps INTPs be more patient, thorough, consistent, and effective in their work.

While flow is closely related to the process mindset, they are not quite synonymous. One can approach an activity with a process mindset without immediately experiencing flow. It typically takes some time to fall into a deep state of flow. For instance, writers know all too well that when they sit down to write, flow is by no means a given. Something needs to "click" in the mind before their writing starts becoming more fluid and seamless. And while it is never guaranteed, in a given instance, that one will achieve a deep state of flow, a process mindset significantly improves the likelihood.

Handling Impediments to Flow

Despite its many benefits, there are a number of reasons INTPs may struggle to find flow. First, because flow entails a substantial perceiving element and INTPs lead with judging (Ti), INTPs must be willing and able to cede some measure of Ti control to experience flow. Readers who have spent any amount of time playing basketball have probably discovered how over-thinking (Ti) a shot disrupts its natural flow and effectiveness. While Ti certainly needs to be involved in gauging a shot (similar to our hammer-nail example in Chapter 1), there are other elements (especially S elements) involved with the shot that will be hindered by Ti micro-management. The same is true in ideational activities. While Ti will play a role, other functions, especially Ne, must be granted sufficient freedom for flow to occur.

INTPs who are strongly driven by ego-ambitions and external rewards will also have a harder time finding flow. Ambition and competition engender a sense of urgency and anxiety that runs counter to the process mindset required to procure flow. Therefore, INTPs must either find a way of reducing their concerns about outcomes or be capable of suspending such concerns when engaging in their work.

Tension & Anxiety

When entering into a session of creative work, the optimal state of mind and body can generally be described as "alert, yet centered and relaxed." But when INTPs are tense or anxious, they are apt to feel hurried, impatient, distracted, and uncentered. Thus, in order to consistently find flow, they must learn to effectively manage tension and anxiety.

Tension is both a mental and physical phenomenon. When answers or solutions (J) don't come as quickly as INTPs expect or desire, their natural response is to tense-up. Those who survey their body may notice, for instance, that their legs are tensed and pulling toward each other, as if trying to "pull together" or "squeeze out" an answer. This is the embodiment of their implicit J belief that straining or trying harder will expedite the desired result.

INTPs typically house ample tension throughout their bodies, much of which they are unaware of. While often belied by their outer adaptability (Ne), INTPs are among the most tense and high-strung of all the types. This is unsurprising when we consider that Ti strives to control and regulate every aspect of INTPs' existence. Their tension may also stem from an ever-present compulsion to find themselves, as well as from external demands and obligations (e.g., children, relationships, financial concerns, etc.).

Since INTPs' purpose is their lifeblood and is therefore not negotiable, the first step in controlling their tension and anxiety often involves reducing their external obligations. In paring down their obligations to a bare minimum, INTPs afford themselves more time to pursue their core interests and experience flow.

In addition to minimizing external demands, INTPs may explore various self-help strategies for controlling tension and anxiety. Cognitive strategies are often atop their list, which we will discuss below. INTPs who are open to mind-body approaches may find practices like yoga surprisingly helpful. Yoga can furnish them with greater awareness of their bodily tension, as well as effective methods for releasing it. "Awareness through movement" exercises, as used by Feldenkrais practitioners, can also prove helpful in this regard. As INTPs release more of their long-held bodily tensions, they feel more calm, centered, and relaxed, as well as less impulsive / compulsive, which makes it easier for them to focus and find flow.

Attention to other factors, such as optimizing the work environment (e.g., reducing noise and distractions), getting plenty of sleep, and regulating caffeine intake, is also important. In striving to maximize their productivity and efficiency, it is easy for INTPs to become caffeine junkies.[9] While it is true that flow requires a certain level of alertness and stimulation, high doses of caffeine can actually prove counterproductive, impairing INTPs' ability to relax, attune to process, and experience flow.

Disruptive Thoughts

Most INTPs are aware of the potentially deleterious effects of negative thoughts on their state of being. In some cases, a single unopposed negative thought may be enough to tank their energy and motivation. Disruptive thoughts can also ramp-up tension and anxiety, making it all the more critical for INTPs to develop effective methods for dealing with them.

One approach involves detaching from the negative thought and allowing it to recede into the background of the mind. Practices like meditation can be helpful in this respect, training the mind to let go of, or avoid attaching to, disruptive thoughts. Attending to bodily sensations, including surveying and releasing muscular tensions, is another helpful technique, removing the focus from the disruptive thought and promoting relaxation.

Another strategy is prioritization, which is particularly useful when a disruptive thought must at some point be dealt with, but not immediately. In such instances, INTPs might record the thought on a "to-do list" to avoid forgetting and worrying about it, which allows them to return their focus to the task at hand.

INTPs may also benefit from cognitive strategies geared toward questioning the logic, truth, or utility of their disruptive thoughts. For instance, if they can demonstrate a given thought or fear to be irrational, or simply recognize when there is nothing they can do to change it (e.g., as would be true of a past event), the thought typically loses much of its power.

Avoiding triggers of disruptive thoughts is another viable strategy. I long ago discovered the benefit of resisting the urge to check my email or blog feedback before I begin writing in the morning. While these things have the potential to provide positive Fe fuel, I found they could also sink my spirit in times I needed it most. This could also serve as an example of prioritization, of recognizing what is most important and determining the optimal sequence for handling one's obligations.

Sleep is another simple yet surprisingly effective way of dealing with negative thoughts (and moods). It furnishes the subconscious with a focused block of time to work through difficult problems and concerns.

Finally, many INTPs find that simply diving into their work (assuming it is stimulating and meaningful) can help subdue disruptive thoughts and anxieties. Engaging in their work and pursuing their interests is one of the most common tactics INTPs employ to escape their troubles and experience flow.

Integration

In *The 16 Personality Types*, I describe flow as the *experience of integration*. From a type perspective, integration typically requires prior differentiation and development of one's four functions, as well as the ability to employ them in a seamless fashion (i.e., flow) and at the appropriate time (i.e., discernment). In addition, those who have reached the integration phase of type development (Phase III) have typically clarified their identity and purpose.

With that said, not all INTPs undergo integration at the same time of life. In fact, some may never reach Phase III (at least not permanently), spending the majority of their years in Phase II. Conversely, those born with "old souls" may integrate at a rather young age. Such INTPs may be endowed with an unusually calm and focused mind, as well as a relative lack of concern for proving themselves to the world, allowing them to more easily adopt a process-oriented mindset. INTPs with an "average-aged soul" are typically at least warming-up to the prospect of integration by mid-life.

Culture and personal circumstances may also affect the timing of integration. We might predict, for instance, that INTPs with more financial security and leisure time would have a greater likelihood of advancing in their personal development. The same might be said of those with access to more educational resources and effective role models. Having at least one N parent, especially a well-integrated NT type, may prove particularly valuable.

Clearly, there is much about integration, as well as type development in general, that falls outside the bounds of INTPs' control. It is largely genes, circumstances, and the subconscious that dictate the course and speed of their development. Since differentiation must precede integration, the latter in many respects hinges on the former. Moreover, there are a number of wonderful elements of the differentiation phase that can be valued and savored in their own right. Hence, there is no need for INTPs to try to rush their transition from Phase II to

Phase III. Instead, they are wise to balance intentionality and striving (J) with an attitude of acceptance and appreciation (P) toward their current stage of development.

Integrating INTPs have a real shot at *mastery* in their interest area. If we consider the body of work produced by Copleston, Kant, or Einstein, we see INTPs who have truly achieved mastery. Of course, both Kant and Einstein were also endowed with extraordinary genius, so we must be cautious in using them as examples, lest we set our bar too high. Nevertheless, recognizing the relationship between integration and mastery can serve as a healthy incentive for INTPs who might be otherwise apathetic toward integration.

In earlier chapters, we discussed the fact that freedom and emancipation are powerful motivators for INTPs. In Chapter 8, we explored approaches that may augment INTPs' sense of philosophical freedom. In Chapter 14, we examined strategies for circumventing left-brain messages that may oppress or impair their ideational freedom and openness. Here, I would like to add integration to the INTP's list of freedom-enhancers. Integrating INTPs have typically liberated themselves from many of the worries and concerns that formerly affected them. The more worries and anxieties they shed, the more readily and routinely they experience the freedom of flow. And the more they find flow, the less their fears and anxieties are reinforced. This allows integrating INTPs to enjoy a greater measure of freedom and clarity of mind.

Closing Thoughts

Over the last three chapters, we have explored and addressed some of the most salient existential problems that INTPs encounter later in their development, as well as ways they might effectively handle them. We've seen how ideals become less potent for INTPs as they progress in their quest, which can lead to perceived shortages in meaning and energy. While this can be a profoundly unsettling and disorienting experience for INTPs, it is fortunate that, during this same time of life, INTPs are being prepared for a different mode of operating, one that involves increased attention to their way of being and how they approach their work. As they become more familiar and skilled with this approach, they discover its capacity for supplying a consistent, even if subtle, stream of meaning and energy. This helps assuage their concerns about meaning and energy, and also furnishes the necessary conditions for INTPs to effectively and consistently carry out their purpose.

To be clear, adopting a process mindset doesn't mean that the content of their work will no longer prove important or relevant to INTPs. Nor does it mean that ideas will no longer play a foundational role in their life and work. Remember, in order to find flow, the activity must be sufficiently stimulating, especially with respect to the dominant and auxiliary functions. Therefore, the frequency of integrating INTPs' engagement with ideas typically remains relatively unchanged. What changes in Phase III is the nature and quality of their approach, that is, the manner in which they work with ideas. Their expectations will also differ in that integrating INTPs no longer need or expect idea-related "highs." Rather than experiencing extreme highs and lows, their energy levels tend to be more consistent and less volatile.

Notes

1. Here, I am referring to ego in the negative sense (e.g., ego-defensive, egotistical, arrogant, prideful, etc.) rather than its Freudian sense.

2. As many spiritual teachers have noted, the diminishment of the ego is a central factor in both moral and spiritual development. As the ego diminishes, there is a commensurate increase in a host of virtues such as patience, humility, self-control, kindness, empathy, etc. Unfortunately, as Jesus and other great sages knew all too well, many religious teachers and authorities fail to understand this basic psychospiritual truth. Instead of identifying and addressing the deep roots (e.g., the ego) of psychospiritual problems, they condemn and war against superficial symptoms (e.g., "sins" and "vices"), which typically yields less than stellar results.

3. I see Being and reality as essentially synonymous, although Being places more emphasis on the subjective element. We can experience a fuller and more meaningful sense of what it feels like to be when we orient ourselves to the present. According to Tillich, it is this meaningful encounter with Being that serves as the foundation for the religious attitude.

4. Closely related to, if not synonymous with, a present / presence-orientation is the practice of mindfulness, which involves attending to the subtle pleasures of life that are ever-present both within (e.g., feelings, bodily sensations, etc.) and without (e.g., those in the surrounding environment), and doing so with an attitude of gratefulness and appreciation. Pirsig's notion of quality is also relevant here, since a quality-oriented mindset is both mindful and tuned-in to the present moment.

5. For mnemonic purposes, it may be worth highlighting that three key notions for integrating INTPs start with the letter "p": present / presence, process, and perceiving.

6. Obituary: The Reverend Frederick Copleston. *Independent.* Feb 4, 1994.

7. It's not that seekers are incapable of adopting a process mindset, but they do seem less likely to do so. Seekers want to find their purpose as quickly as possible which, at least on the surface, doesn't square well with a process mindset. INTPs who have identified their purpose, by contrast, may see the process mindset as pragmatically necessary for effectively navigating their new sphere of existence.

8. Killingsworth, M. "Does Mind-Wandering Make You Unhappy?" *Greater Good.* July 16, 2013.

9. While I am unaware of any studies to this effect, I've noticed that types with a dominant judging function (i.e., IPs and EJs) tend to prefer stimulants, which are felt to enhance their J propensities (e.g., productivity, efficiency). Types with a dominant perceiving function (EPs and IJs), by contrast, often prefer cannabis or depressants (e.g., alcohol), which seem to augment their natural perceptive process. I've read accounts of IP writers, for instance, who are coffee addicts or even use drugs like cocaine. Some IJ writers, such as Stephen King (INTJ), have been known to abuse alcohol. Considering that INTPs are naturally rather high-strung, they may find it helpful to significantly reduce their caffeine intake, especially when performing creative work. Doing so may help them reduce anxiety and more easily find flow.

CLOSING REMARKS

INTPs seek a purpose that is meaningful, important, and can serve as a lifelong source of interest and investment. In tandem with Ne, Ti compels INTPs to seek their purpose by way of the mind. It urges them to establish a clear, firm, and foundational understanding of themselves, their purpose, their worldview, and their philosophy of life. Without an adequate understanding of these matters, INTPs know that committing to a purpose would be arbitrary, inauthentic, and ultimately futile.

Over the course of this book, we have explored a number of ideas and approaches that INTPs might incorporate into their understanding. We began by considering the ways in which their four functions might shape and impact their purpose. This was premised on the idea that purpose is a natural outflow of the self. So by understanding themselves and their personality type, INTPs can gain a better sense of their purpose. Incorporating knowledge of their functions into a general conception of their purpose, INTPs might view themselves as independent creatives, innovators, explorers, investigators, philosophers, and if we factor in Si, scholars or historians. Despite being rather broad and vague, these sorts of notions can help INTPs envision their general role in the world.

INTPs may also seek their purpose by way of core concepts. They sense that identifying the concepts that are consistently interesting and meaningful to them might point the way to their purpose. As examples, we discussed Pirsig's concept of quality and Tillich's notion of ultimate concern. If we were to consult INTP philosophers, we would discover that concepts like freedom, spirit, life, mind, and Being are often on center stage. From this we can see that INTPs gravitate toward concepts that are broad, versatile, and can speak to metaphysical realities. Not only do such concepts point to INTPs' ultimate concerns, but their breadth and versatility grant their Ne the freedom it needs to explore and imagine.

While INTPs' quest for purpose is largely abstract in nature, what INTPs are ultimately seeking in a purpose is more concrete. Namely, they seek a meaningful craft and interest area. A craft provides the forum required for INTPs to shape, express, and give form to their ideas. It grants them opportunities to invest themselves in a focused fashion and to make tangible contributions to society, thereby reconciling their I and E needs. Ideally, their craft (e.g., writing, engineering, coding, etc.) will consistently engage their top two functions, Ti and Ne. In many cases, their chosen interest area, which supplies the ideational content for their craft, will incorporate Fe.

Although INTPs may never reach a point of absolute certainty regarding their purpose, they must at some point make an educated decision to embrace and invest in something. INTPs who fail to invest themselves in a purpose may never feel fully satisfied with their lives. Typically, INTPs in their thirties or forties will have amassed sufficient life experience to discern the nature of their core interests. By reflecting on their past (Si), they can identify recurrent beliefs, skills, and interests that can serve as the foundation for their purpose moving forward.

As discussed at various points in this book, INTPs must undergo differentiation (i.e., clarify their identity and purpose) prior to integration, which is why most INTPs, especially in the first half of life, prioritize the former. Indeed, some INTPs seem to discover integration almost accidentally, as the forces of life render them more humble and patient human beings. Other INTPs may integrate out of practical necessity. No longer capable of relying on big dreams, ideals, or ego aspirations to motivate them, they turn to integrative practices as a means of navigating their post-idealist existence. Specifically, adopting a present / process-oriented mindset can furnish the energy and meaning they need to successfully enact their purpose, even apart from big ideals. So while integration is often associated with moral or spiritual development, for many INTPs it is a matter of utility, a tool for carrying out their purpose and cultivating a satisfying life. With that said, integrating INTPs have typically become more virtuous, which suggests they have also progressed on a moral plane, even if somewhat inadvertently. This observation is highlighted in Pirsig's book, which shows that in cultivating the right mindset in one's work, one is also learning *how to live*. In other words, the optimal mindset for quality work and a well-lived life happens to be one and the same.

As INTPs adopt and grow in this mindset, time plays a diminished role in their thinking. Instead of constantly anticipating and focusing on the future, they become more present-oriented (or presence-oriented). This opens the door to a new type of existence, one that allows them to effectively and appreciatively explore and create within the context of their purpose.

I wish you the best as you move forward in your personal quest.

—*A.J. Drenth*

REFERENCES & RESOURCES

To learn more about INTPs and the other personality types, be sure to visit PersonalityJunkie.com.

Adams, J.L. *Paul Tillich's Philosophy of Culture, Science, and Religion.* Harper & Row. 1965.

Aiken, H. *The Age of Ideology.* Mentor Books. 1956.

Atkins, K. *Self and Subjectivity.* Blackwell. 2005.

Barrett, W. *Irrational Man: A Study in Existential Philosophy.* Anchor. 1990.

Bergson, H. *Creative Evolution.* Barnes & Noble. 2005.

Copleston, F. *A History of Philosophy.* Volume VI. Doubleday. 1960.

Csikszentmihaly, M. *Flow: The Psychology of Optimal Experience.* Harper. 2008.

De Beistegui, M. *Immanence: Deleuze and Philosophy.* Edinburgh University Press. 2010.

Deleuze, G. & Guattari, F. *What is Philosophy?* Columbia University Press. 1994.

Delaporte, F. A *Vital Rationalist: Selected Writings from Georges Canguilhem.* Zone Books. 1994.

Drenth, A.J. *The 16 Personality Types: Profiles, Theory, & Type Development.* Inquire Books. 2013.

Drenth, A.J. *The INTP: Personality, Careers, Relationships, & the Quest for Truth and Meaning.* Inquire Books. 2013.

Drenth, A.J. *My True Type: Clarifying Your Personality Type, Preferences & Functions.* Inquire Books. 2014.

Gutting, G. *Continental Philosophy of Science.* Blackwell. 2005.

James, W. *Pragmatism.* Dover. 1995.

Jung, C.G. *Psychological Reflections.* Edited by Jacobi, J. Bollingen Foundation. 1953.

Jung, C.G. *Psychological Types.* Princeton University Press. 1971.

Keirsey, D. *Please Understand Me II.* Prometheus. 1998.

Kierkegaard, S. *Concluding Unscientific Postscript.* Princeton University Press. 1941.

Kierkegaard, S. *Either / Or.* Doubleday. 1959.

King, T. *Jung's Four and Some Philosophers: A Paradigm for Philosophy.* University of Notre Dame Press. 1999.

McGilchrist, I. *The Master and His Emissary.* Yale University Press. 2009.

Myers, I.B., et al. *MBTI Manual: A Guide to the Development and Use of the Myers-Briggs Type Indicator.* 1998.

Nietzsche, F. *The Will to Power.* Barnes & Noble. 2006.

Pirsig, R. *Zen and the Art of Motorcycle Maintenance.* Harper Torch. 2006.

Riso, D. & Hudson, R. *Personality Types: Using the Enneagram for Self-Discovery.* Houghton Mifflin. 1996.

Sandoval, JE. *Cognitive Type*. Nemvus. 2016.

Spinoza, B. *Ethics*. Penguin. 1996.

Thomson, L. *Personality Type: An Owner's Manual*. Shambhala. 1998.

Tillich, P. *The Courage to Be*. Yale University. 2000.

Wilber, K. *Sex, Ecology, Spirituality: The Spirit of Evolution*. Shambhala. 1995.

Made in the USA
Lexington, KY
10 September 2019